Who Am I?

Wisconsin Studies in Autobiography

William L. Andrews

General Editor

Who Am I?

AN AUTOBIOGRAPHY OF EMOTION, MIND, AND SPIRIT

Yi-Fu Tuan

The University of Wisconsin Press

The University of Wisconsin Press
2537 Daniels Street
Madison, Wisconsin 53718

3 Henrietta Street
London WC2E 8LU, England

1   3   5   4   2

Printed in the United States of America

Library of Congress Cataloging-in-Publication Data
Tuan, Yi-fu, 1930–
Who am I?: an autobiography of emotion, mind,
and spirit / Yi-fu Tuan.
150 pp.   cm. — (Wisconsin studies in autobiography)
ISBN 0-299-16660-0 (cloth: alk. paper)
1. Tuan, Yi-fu, 1930–   2. Geographers Biography.
3. Chinese Americans Biography.   I. Title.   II. Series.
G69.T84A3   1999
973'.04951'0092—dc21
[B]   99-23672

Contents

Illustrations

Who Am I?

1

Autobiography: My Angle

S OCRATES famously said that the unexamined life is not worth living. But, of course, if one keeps pausing to examine life, one will not live at all. Self-examination must therefore come only at stated intervals, with perhaps a last ruminative survey toward the end of one's life. Now that I am old but still have my wits about me, "Who am I?" is a question that I wish to put to myself before it is too late.

From the experience of wise people like Montaigne, I know that I won't go far with this question—this exercise in self-examination—if I just withdraw into my study and reflect. That way leads to phantoms. The self is only knowable through a sustained and cumulative mental effort, the most efficient form of which is writing. Writing produces a work. I now know myself through a work. Is it a true reflection of my real self? That question too seems to lead to phantoms. *True* and *real* are tricky words. Little is to be gained by grappling with them in an autobiography, unless one is a metaphysician and enjoys subtleties piled on subtleties almost for their own sake. Like most people, I am probably a compound of selves, but there is only one self—the one embodied in this work—that I can truly be said to know.

Now that I know, is there any point in telling what I know to others? Socrates doesn't say, although I can imagine him saying, "Self-knowledge is its own reward. Wanting to pass it on to others is vanity, like talking at length about oneself at a party." I see that. Nevertheless, an alternative position is possible. Yes, an element of vanity is indubitably there: one wants to be thought well of, if not for outward accomplishments, then for the depth of one's self-understanding. But it is not all vanity. Wanting to communicate has a strong psychological justification. For if casual self-examination can only lead to phantoms, sustained and disciplined self-examination can still seem a little unreal unless it jells into a written work

3

that can be read, mulled over, and understood by another individual. This is because we, as social beings through and through, need confirmation by others in order to know who we are. But the self that others confirm in everyday life is a rather shallow person constructed from a limited range of habits and customs that society openly favors. Will the deeper and more complex self revealed in serious reflection also meet with approval, or will it elicit surprise and consternation? Much as I have always wanted a frank answer, it is only now, with the courage of second childhood or the indifference of approaching senility, that I dare to countenance—well, what? Not harsh judgment, for the circle I move in is far too enlightened for that, but rather an awkwardly polite inching away, the slightest dip in social temperature, shifts in behavior and mood so minimal and subtle that they are easily relegated to the basement of consciousness.

"Who am I?" is a fashionable question at the close of the millennium. Everyone seems to be asking it. Not only individuals but groups and even nations ask themselves "who am I?" or "who are we?" Among the major causes of a weakening sense of self are social and geographical mobility and rapid technological change. We are, as pundits say, in the midst of an identity crisis. Biographies and autobiographies abound. Self-revelations of a boastful kind arrive not only from the famous but ordinary folk and attract high ratings in the media. As a rootless person, I am a natural for self-examination, and this could lead, given the spirit of the times, to self-exposure through a variety of means, including that of autobiography. It may be that I am especially tempted, for I am rootless in more than one sense. I never lived in one place for more than five years until, at age thirty-eight, I moved to Minneapolis. Before that, I was constantly changing residence, first as a child with my family, then alone as an adult. One city after another was called "home": Tianjin, Nanjing, Shanghai, Kunming, Chongqing, Canberra, Sydney, Manila, London, Oxford, Paris, Berkeley, Bloomington (Indiana), Chicago, Albuquerque, and Toronto. Fourteen years in Minneapolis and another fourteen in Madison, my current place of residence, are the only source of any rooted feeling I may have. Socially, I am likewise adrift and for a simple reason—I am single. The one portable soil—family—in which an individual is given natural grounding is not available to me.

How does my situation compare with that of others? By others, I have in mind first the people I know in daily life, mostly American friends. Their backgrounds differ: some have shown a far greater inclination to move from place to place, but even the most mobile are more plugged into society and the world than I, if only because they have spouses and offspring, and, with them, necessary ties to neighborhood, school, and other local institutions. By others, I also have in mind total strangers—people who live elsewhere in the world or have lived in earlier times. Their sense of self, as recorded by ethnographers and historians, provides me with the broadest possible backdrop against which to raise the question of my own selfhood.

First, then, the Americans. As I remember it, not so long ago the question "Who am I?" seldom came up. When it did, most men would probably have answered with a profession (plumber, lawyer) and most women with the family (wife of a plumber, mother of four children). Since the sixties, however, not only is the question raised more often but the old answer is no longer considered adequate. An individual requires a past, not just the present and a future, and an ancestral line, not just current family, to produce a solid sense of self. The search for ancestors and the old homestead, for cultural heritage, for things that are reassuringly fixed because they belong to the past, becomes a hobby as well as a serious attempt at discovering one's identity; this is so not only with the old and the middle aged but even with the young, who thereby risk losing that quality of starry-eyed hopefulness that was once the unmistakable hallmark of young Americans.

Does digging into the past really give men and women of our time a sense of identity and belonging? Perhaps, but the identity and belonging so gained are effects of *present* activity, present research into and present reconstruction of the past, and not a reimmersion in the past, which of course is impossible. The idea that one is able to return to an earlier time, to feel again the communal bond that existed then, is an illusion. But a powerful illusion can seem real, and maybe that is all that people in our fissiparous postmodern world need.

What is not an illusion is the force of communal bonding in premodern times, among preliterate and nonliterate peoples. For the nostalgic modern man and woman, then, the question to be honestly confronted is: "If a reimmersion in the past is possible, do I really want it? Have I any clear idea what it is like to be so identified with the group that my individual self becomes almost a phantom?" The world's ethnographic literature is so rich in strange habits and customs that most readers do not consider the virtual disappearance of the self in the group as anything special. But to one reader—me!—it is, and perhaps that says something about me. In any case, as a young student reading such literature, I could hardly credit anthropologist Dorothy Lee's account of the Wintu Indians of northern California, for whom, apparently, the self is not so much a bounded entity as a concentration that gradually fades at the edges and gives way to other entities. The Wintu do not, for example, "use *and* when referring to individuals who are, or live or act together." They prefer to say *John we*, using

5

John as a specification, rather than *John and I*, where the *we* is exposed as made up of two separate individuals. And what happens when Lee asks a Wintu woman, Sadie Marsh, for her autobiography? Predictably, she tells a story about someone else—her first husband. When Lee insists on Sadie's own history, she proceeds to tell what she calls "my story" but about the first three quarters of it are occupied with the lives of her grandfather, her uncle, and her mother before her birth.[1]

Certain nonliterate peoples do have a strong sense of self and of individual differences. The Tswana of east Africa, for example, say that even children born of the same parents are more different than they are alike, especially in thought and feeling. But individuality, while clearly recognized, is feared rather than admired. It is suppressed, for beyond the recognition of individuality is the far keener awareness that an individual who stands alone, or who stands out in the group, is vulnerable.[2] What is distinctive of Europeans, by comparison with other peoples, is this. From the sixteenth century onward, not only was there a growing recognition of individuality but a steady accretion of pride in it. First, family portraits were painted; then, increasingly, portraits of individuals and self-portraits; biographies, autobiographies, and reflexive essays (outstandingly, Montaigne's) were written. Of course, only people of substance could command and only people of talent could engage in these enterprises.[3] Interestingly, many biographies and autobiographies produced before 1900 and even thereafter showed a note of uncertainty in that their authors seemed to want their subjects to be both unique and to have that uniqueness submerged in the categories of respectable society, past and present. And so, like the Wintu woman, they might spend inordinate space depicting parents, uncles and aunts, and their social worlds before introducing the distinctive self.

Even Americans, self-proclaimed individualists, were and probably still are more inclined to write family histories than autobiographies. Some of my retired colleagues, I note, use their research skills to reconstruct their genealogical pasts. Typically, they trace their roots to Europe, envisage the epic journey of their ancestors across the Atlantic, the struggle for survival in a city of the eastern seaboard, the establishment of a comfortable foothold in a middle western farm, and then the story of their own generation—the births of siblings and cousins, their childhoods and early schooling. What surprises me is that most family histories end at this juncture. Why is this? Why stop just when information is sufficient to allow the depiction of fully rounded human individuals? A plausible answer is that, whereas life in the old country can seem romantic, the trip over the ocean epical, the struggles of forebears in the New World heroic, and early schooling nostalgic, the subsequent path of adulthood is, by comparison, commonplace—a succession of unexceptional family events, job changes, and promotions; these are not worth writing about or are worth writing about only to family members and close friends.

Such reflections have convinced me that most human beings, despite a tendency to boast a little in conversation, in family circulars, or even (if opportunity offers) in a three-minute call to a radio talk show, are fundamentally modest. When the self-knowledge they seek and find becomes compendious, they do not seek to thrust it on others. Am I, then, an exception? What is my excuse, since I am without the sort of fame, notoriety, or exceptional life circumstance that might justify biographical or autobiographical treatment? The best answer should be the completed work itself. But I have a more general answer or maybe simply a conviction (partly religious), which is this: just as no human life is negligible, so no human life story is negligible, not worth telling. If a story seems a bore, the fault lies in the arrangement of words, not in the life. Critical, then, is the availability of a talented narrator. Am I such a one? Do I, for a start, have a good memory? Bad memory can be compensated by hard research. What is my attitude toward hard research—toward foraging among old letters and digging into public archives in the absence of which an autobiography can seem lightweight?

As autobiographer, I confess to several weaknesses, most especially a poor memory. I can remember little of the first ten years of my life, which I spent in China. I have a better haul of images from Australia, where I lived from the ages of ten through fifteen, but it remains meager. The six months in the Philippines are quite vivid, and from 1946 onward—from age fifteen onward—I can say that the details I am able to recall are at last respectably dense.

Doubts about my memory came to me in late middle age, when my brother Tai-Fu began to reminisce nostalgically about his childhood and mine. I have always been impressed by how much he can recall. Yet he is older than I by only one year. After a two-month visit to China in 1997, he returned to the United States full of stories of the village we lived in, the school we attended, sixty years ago. He contacted his childhood schoolmates. He remembers their names, what they were like, what he and they did together. Why can't I do the same? Why have I forgotten so much? Does this forgetfulness explain my lack of desire to return to China, for what's the point of visiting a landscape of memory that is so impoverished?

Teasingly, I say to Tai-Fu that the reason he remembers so much and I so little is that he is a pessimist, whereas I am an optimist. A pessimist puts his golden age in the past, an optimist puts his in the future. I may have deliberately buried my store of childhood experiences so that I won't be tempted to stay there, so that I can be more accepting of the present and acquire an outlook toward the future that is hopeful rather than anxious.

My need to have a hopeful outlook toward the future may also have affected my understanding of the human past in general. I have not ignored the human past. On the contrary, I enjoy reading history. But my reading may have been selective, for from history books I gain the strong impression that earlier times could be pretty awful even in the midst of genuine achievements. When people today feel disgusted with the desecration of nature and the erection of meretricious or ugly buildings on its scarred back, they tend to seek vindication and reassurance from a golden age of long ago. Some find it in the eighteenth century (before the Industrial Revolution), some in the Middle Ages, some in classical antiquity, some in even mistier landscapes. The further back they go, the more likely it is that the perfection they locate there is a product of wishful thinking. Although that is not at all how I view the past, I was for a time ready to agree with Jacquetta Hawkes that eighteenth-century England might just be what people are looking for, if only from an aesthetic and ecological point of view. In that century, Englishmen possessed the land without committing outrages against it. Rich and poor alike "knew how to use the stuff of their countryside to raise comely buildings and to group them with distinctive grace. Town and country having grown up together to serve one another's needs now enjoyed a moment of balance."[4]

But that was my first impression. With a closer look, I began to see a more piebald picture, as did other writers, though not (it would seem) Hawkes herself. For example, in his biography of Samuel Johnson, John Wain wrote longingly of lovely landscapes in Johnson's time that have since disappeared. However, in the midst of the praise he had to acknowledge that they had a strikingly incongruous and somewhat sinister element, namely, a large number of diseased and disfigured human beings and animals.[5] Another egregious blemish, which surprisingly few landscape historians have dwelt on, was the large number of gibbets on which the tarred corpses of criminals were displayed. Whenever possible, the gibbets were located on prominences and at crossroads to achieve maximum visibility. Timid travelers made detours around them, especially during dark nights.[6]

I confessed earlier that I might have repressed my childhood experiences, especially the good ones, so as to allow a more genial view of my later years. I may have played the same trick on human history; that is, to feel comfortable with the present and entertain hope for the future, I may have read into human history a broadly progressive trend that many sophisticated historians disallow. I have persuaded myself of the existence of progress by envisioning the social position I would have had to occupy in order to feel content in successively earlier times. I conclude that in the eighteenth century, I would have to have been a squire with sizable land holdings; in the Middle Ages, a great baron; and in ancient Egypt, no less than the pharaoh himself.

I can enjoy history even when its reports are grim because history, as presented to me by historians, is not (it hardly needs be said) the past but rather a colorful landscape—delusively complete—that lies before me and that I can explore appreciatively or critically with my mind's eye. My own past, not having been reordered by a historian, is not a landscape. Like all pasts, it is a thin spread of oddments, piled high here and there, that happens to have survived. A traditional autobiographer would consider it his task to file them in separate categories and time slots and in one way or another dress them up so that, together, they have a semblance of completion, of being a finished landscape or an unbroken story line. But I am not such an autobiographer. I cannot be a proper historian of my own past because I cannot bear to look at the material remains, which have for me an indescribable air of sadness. Perversely perhaps, threadbare jeans, chewing gum hardened by age, rusted paper clips, and stained high-school and college diplomas speak of immense loss rather than survival. The *pastness* of the past causes me bewilderment and, at times, a feeling akin to nausea.

Strange to say, ideas and theories of the past do not distress me by their pastness. For example, when I open Thomas Burnet's book, *The Theory of the Earth* (1684), I am aware of the musty smell coming out of its yellowed pages, I am aware that its author has long ago returned to dust. But the ideas in the book, quaintly dated as they may be, are still a flaming of the human spirit that inspires. Ideas are of their time yet transcend it. I see them this way because they are not like matter, which decays, or worse, like biological matter, which enters into a stage of putrescence before turning into minerals. I am not temperamentally equipped to be a historian of material life, but I can be a historian of the spirit. And by spirit, I mean the whole range of mental and psychological capabilities, including not only ideas, thoughts, and philosophies but also the tone and coloring of experience in all its variety. It surprises me that though my factual memory is poor, my memory of the psychological character, or mood, of past events is extraordinarily vivid.

Thus readers are forewarned of this work's shortcomings. They will not find the compendious factual information, firm chronological arc, and highlighting of the more public events that many memoirs provide. And yet, paradoxically, one of the work's merits is that it *has* these shortcomings. The fact is, a fat volume ill suits my personality; a sense of progression is necessarily weak in my life for lack of such powerful springboards as courtship, marriage, birth of children, and so on; last, an introvert much prefers home entertainment—the compact videos of his own mind—to the hurly-burly public events of the wide screen.

Besides these "shortcomings," which I now regard as negative merit, I can also point to some of the work's positive qualities. I can claim that it is the first autobiography ever written by a middle-class Chinese American geographer. The claim is bolder than it sounds, for the combination of "middle-class Chinese" and "geographer" makes the writing of autobiography most unlikely. Either one alone would deter the venture. A middle-class Chinese such as myself cannot offer the attractive and highly marketable theme of struggle and heroic climb from Chinatown poverty to suburban affluence. For I had no such struggle and climb. Chinese immigrants who were middle-class professionals have always been accepted and successful in the United States. And what is more boring than a story of unqualified success—from good student to well-paid engineer? As for that other category, "geographer," into which I fall, most geographers are too extroverted, too happily engaged with external reality, to write their life stories. And so the field is left open to me: a middle-class Chinese, yes, but one who in his lifelong bachelordom is obliged, on that account alone, to live outside the Chinese social fold; a geographer, yes, but a maverick in the discipline to the degree that, unlike most other geographers, my landscapes are "inscapes," as much psychological conditions as material arrangements.

What else is distinctive about my autobiography? Another mark of distinction, I suggest, is that it records an unusual overall direction or movement in life. For most people, life moves from private to public—from a childhood spent in the home and neighborhood to an adulthood spent in public forums of increasing scope: local, regional, national. My life, by contrast, has moved in the opposite direction—from public to private, from world to self. It has always seemed to me that my childhood was public. Its stage was the Chinese nation and the world. It could seem that way for two reasons. One was the drama of the war with Japan followed by the Second World War. These wars impinged directly on my family and on me. The other was my father's position in Chinese society: though an official of the middle rank even at the zenith of his career, he was nevertheless a member of the elite at a time when the educated class was small.

By the time I turned into a young adult, World War II had ended. Events in the world no longer impinged on me quite so directly. My life became private, my world shrank to the various campuses at which I studied or worked. Meanwhile, at these sheltered campuses, my mental life was able to expand. Self-examination has made me more aware of who I am; examination has made me more aware of the nature of external reality. These activities continued into middle age and old age. And so the direction of my life is not quite from public to private. In its mature half, I have been able to regain the world, though it is one of ideas and thought rather than one of action and events.

This spiraling path provides the autobiography with a temporal structure that it would otherwise lack. And so, following the introduction, I turn to "World Stage and Public Events," and then to two chapters of increasing subjectivity: if the one is personal, the other is intimate. When I wrote earlier that even the ordinary life experiences of an ordinary individual should have general interest and import, I had this core section of my autobiography in mind. By contrast, "Salvation by Geography" is both more individualistic, being an account of my own contributions to geography, and a return to the wider world.

2

World Stage and Public Events

S A CHILD, I keenly felt the impact of national and world events even though I could not grasp their importance. As an adult, I can far better grasp their importance, but they have become for me forces and personalities "out there" that I know about only through the media. As a child, I was patted on the head or given toys by a few men who played significant roles in Chinese national life and at least one who became a world figure. As an adult, I have not known the movers and shakers personally, and what influence I have on the great world is restricted to a scattering of people, widely dispersed, who share my interest in the human habitat.

How come this trajectory? One factor was simply the historical accident of being born at a certain time. The first twenty years of my existence (1930–1950) just happened to be full of the sort of events that made front-page headlines. They included, most notably, the Sino-Japanese War and the Second World War, decolonization, and the founding of the United Nations—and with it the possibility of a brave new world. Events of this magnitude necessarily touched people's lives, including that of a Chinese child, whereas the more muddled, comparatively slighter events of the century's last forty years could not. When I, a nine-year-old, heard that, to appease the Japanese, the British had closed the Burma Road, China's only lifeline to the outside world, the watermelon cubes in my glass—the ultimate summer treat for a boy—suddenly tasted flat. I held on to the glass and stared at it without comprehension. My world had come to an end.

Years later, as a college teacher in the United States, even the Cuban crisis of 1962, which could have triggered a nuclear Armageddon, was not real enough for me to postpone my geomorphological field trip, though I did remark to a colleague, as I piled food and water into the vehicle in preparation for three days in the desert, that I might return to a radioactive Albuquerque. A year after the crisis, the superpowers were still at logger-heads. I went to see a movie on Central Avenue, Albuquerque's main street. Emerging from the cinema, I saw search lights sweeping the night sky and immediately concluded that an air raid was in progress. Fear of violent death, which I thought I had put behind me, returned in a sickening rush. It took me a moment or two to realize that the lights advertised a forthcoming motorcar show at the local colosseum. What a relief—but also, now that I think of it, what a comedown! As a child, I was targeted for destruction by imperial Japan; as an adult, my wallet was targeted for thinning by motorcar corporations. That, in a nutshell, is the difference between being on a world stage, if only as a nameless victim, and being a teacher in a quiet New Mexico town, lured by search lights to attend a sales show, where the stakes would be whether I would buy a Ford or a Chevy.

My sense of being on a world stage in the 1930s owed only in part to the great national and world events. In greater and more active part, it was a consequence of my status as a child of middle-class professionals. Such a child, if he had any talent and ambition, could well see himself as a future player in the world, even when in actual fact he lived with his family in poverty in a country devastated by war.

How could mere middle-class status confer such presumption of self-worth? The term *middle class* is problematic, so broad and loose that it is almost meaningless unless it is placed in a specific context. I use it because my father, who was exposed to and influenced by American class terminology, found it serviceable, as did his friends and colleagues who had some schooling abroad. *Scholar-gentry* is narrower and sharper and might seem better suited to the Chinese situation, but it too has its problems. It is a dated category, flavored by a past that was gone before my childhood arrived. Moreover, the word *gentry* has an unavoidably British ring and evokes land-ownership and elegant country-house living, which does not fit my family history or the history of most Chinese families that owned fewer than twenty acres. So I shall make do with *middle class*, giving it a more focused and specialized meaning by saying that, yes, of course, it included merchants and the better-off farmers. But by the critical tests of social centrality and political power, it meant, first and foremost, a tiny group of well-educated and well-trained men, who in addition to classical Chinese learning had some educational experience in a foreign country. The members of this group, their families, and hangers-on enjoyed not only social prestige but also political influence that reached well beyond local to regional and even national spheres.

My father came from an impoverished family. He had to struggle as a boy. He went to school on a scholarship. Still, impoverished or not, he had the confidence of his class. When we were children, he might speak to us about great wealth and power but as things to avoid, not to acquire, because they tended to corrupt. As a government functionary, Father recognized official superiors but not social superiors. Not recognizing social superiors made people like my father feel egalitarian and democratic; at times they took "middle" to mean less a position in a hierarchy than a sort of golden mean to which all could and should aspire. Americans who saw this streak of egalitarian idealism in the Chinese admired them for it, all the more so when the Americans compared the layered but not rigidly stratified Chinese society with India's caste system and the highly stratified society of Japan.

Father's moral and social values were essentially Confucian. Born in 1899, he could have lived in any Chinese century. His ideal was a scholar-official whose life exemplified probity and learning. To this was added a Western layer, made up of democracy, Deweyan pragmatism, and science, that he acquired in the mid-1920s as a graduate student in the United States. Like his classmates, Father rose quickly to positions of influence once he returned to China. How bland my own early career now seems compared with Father's at the same stage. In my thirties, I moved from an assistant to an associate professorship. Father, in his thirties, was at various times and sometimes simultaneously a university teacher of foreign languages, the director of Beijing's public telephone and telegraph company, the private secretary of a northern warlord, and an official in the ministry of foreign affairs. For him, it was routine to meet with foreigners and to do business in four languages—Chinese, English, French, and German—every day. He was a cosmopolitan, I was a provincial.

But as a child, I participated in his cosmopolitan world. I acquired an early self-confidence that shielded me against racial slurs or tempered their sting, when we moved to Australia and then England and when I came to study in the United States. Only late in life did I wonder about the sources of this self-confidence. The event that, more than any other, made me so wonder was the single-minded pursuit of ethnic pride in the United States from the 1970s onward. Ethnics—those of non-European origin in particular—supposedly lacked self-esteem. Whatever pride they had in the home country was eroded when they entered mainstream American society as lowly laborers and workers and when the cultures they brought with them and developed in the new world were judged "folk," "quaint," "backward"—deficient in one way or another. In time, ethnics themselves came to accept these judgments. I am forcefully struck by how far these immigrant experiences differed from my own. The times when my self-esteem plunged could almost always be traced to an acute sense of personal inadequacy. My social background and the cultural baggage I brought from China were, by contrast, sources of strength. They made and continue to make me feel confident and central, even when American society, for its own larger political purposes, chooses to designate me as an ethnic, a minority person, more or less marginalized and so in need of succor.

I suppose I have always known that social status bestows privileges and with them self-confidence. Less clear to me was the role of my cultural background, and least clear was the role that that cultural background could play by virtue of its special character. Only in mature adulthood did I finally see that the pride of culture, which I picked up as a child, was not the pride of customs and mores (eating with chopsticks and such) but rather the pride of "high" culture, national culture, or civilization, an honorific that the Chinese have given themselves but that would be an empty boast if it were not periodically confirmed by outsiders, as it has been throughout history.

How exactly did high culture, national culture, or civilization contribute to a Chinese child's self-esteem? How were messages of China's presumed superiority passed on? Schoolbooks were no doubt an important conduit. Because young children couldn't be expected to understand real history, we were given instead heroic tales drawn from the past. One tale that left a permanent impression on me was that of a Southern Song general, Yueh Fei, who defended the Chinese dynasty against Mongol invaders. Our schoolbook showed a picture of the general kneeling by the side of his mother, who wrote on his bare back the words "Return to us our mountains and rivers." The tale made sense, for we were only too aware of the Japanese military presence. With bombs falling on us daily, patriotic sentiment was easily aroused. But patriotism was not the same as civilizational pride. How civilizational pride was transmitted to us children is more puzzling. In the Yueh Fei story, I suppose it somehow conveyed a message beyond the simple patriotism of us-versus-them—namely, that the Song Chinese were civilized, whereas the Mongol invaders were barbarians. In defending the Song, Yueh Fei was defending not just one country but civilization itself. I can say this: the inculcation of pride was not achieved by simple boasting. It did not resort to chanting a litany of accomplishments, such as we built the Great Wall, we invented gunpowder and the compass, our ships roamed the seas before the Europeans did, and so on. It was less specific. One means was a quiet but persistent assumption of civilizational superiority over the nomads, even though the nomads might be more powerful militarily, as is evident in the Yueh Fei story. But more subtle and (I believe) more effective was the way our role models, parents and teachers, spoke. They sometimes spoke as though they were proponents of human, not just Chinese, civilization.

Could this have been an artful dodge? It was one thing to compare Chinese accomplishments with those of nomadic tribes beyond the Great Wall, but how would Chinese accomplishments measure up against those of Europe and the West? An honest answer could be demoralizing. So, instead of making such spatial comparisons, our educators chose to draw attention to the temporal idea of progress. They said to us children that, yes, we Chinese were ignorant and superstitious in the past, but we know better now, and we will know even more and grow stronger in the future. And so China's humiliating defeat by the British during the Opium War (1839–1842), though mentioned in all history books, as it must be, could be relegated to the status of an incident—a temporary asymmetry of power—that will disappear as the Chinese modernize. Assuming a universalist position also helps. The "we" of schoolbooks is Chinese. But sometimes the pronoun refers to humanity. Humankind as a whole has improved and will continue to improve, even if some parts of it (including China) temporarily lag behind.

Children's classroom learning has to be backed by ordinary, day-to-day experience if it is to take. Mine was. Between the ages of seven and ten, I lived with my family in a village on the outskirts of Chongqing. We were poor. Everyone was who didn't deal in the black market. Our school was a single room attached to an electricity-generating station. To get there we had to pass through a village, which I disliked and feared for its sour odors, the fetid mud that tugged at my shoes, the dark and dank shops with their assortment of sinister wares, and, above all, the occasional funeral procession. I can see even now the procession and its centerpiece—the corpse. It was wrapped in a bamboo sheet, on top of which was tied a rooster, which served as an advance warning system to the carriers and mourners, for it would crow if the corpse stirred. What a happy contrast our school provided! Separated by a mere hundred yards, the village and the school were worlds apart in enlightenment. In the school we read elevating stories from the Chinese, European, and American pasts, stories about great scientists and inventors such as Isaac Newton, Louis Pasteur, and Benjamin Franklin that were meant to stimulate our intellectual ambition, and moral tales—ones of filial piety, naturally, but also Oscar Wilde's "The Happy Prince"—that were intended to help us grow into compassionate adults.

If the cosmopolitan flavor of our education was remarkable, even more so, as I now look back, was the ingenuity with which our elders sought to inspire in us the idea that the search for knowledge was not only noble but fun. Fun? Well, what child wouldn't like to bring down electricity with a kite? If Benjamin Franklin could run around in a storm, why couldn't I do the same—in the interest of science, of course? I liked another story, supposedly taken from the life of the inventor James Watt, even better. Watt's mother asked the boy, whose mind always seemed to be elsewhere, to time the cooking of an egg. A while later, the mother asked, "Well, how is it doing?" The boy looked at the watch in his hand but found, to his bewilderment, an egg! The watch was boiling merrily in the water. How we children must have laughed. Was the teacher encouraging us to be naughty? In a way, yes. That was the wonder of my earliest schooling. The grown-ups who oversaw our education were wise enough to know that naughtiness could be the beginning of discovery and invention. Young Watt didn't intend to do anything silly. His mind just wasn't on the job. So the real message we received was that it was all right to be impractical if one's mind dwelt on higher things.

Even more of a surprise to me now is the inclusion of Wilde's fairy tale in our reading. Chinese lore and literature lack stories of young geniuses who by their brilliance put their elders to shame, the one exception being in the area of poetic creativity. Therefore, borrowing from the West makes sense. But the Chinese have moral tales galore; many emphasize honesty, responsibility, and, above all, filial piety—practices that every society must promote to some extent to function at all. Why, then, "The Happy Prince"—a fable in which self-sacrifice in the succoring of helpless strangers is carried to the point of death and, from the Chinese viewpoint, the even worse fate of social ignominy thereafter? Answer: Chinese moral precepts are deficient in loftiness. Children—maybe all of us—need something a little more uplifting, a little more daring, than a mere spirit of cooperation among family members and neighbors. Buddhism could have provided the missing dimension: children might well appreciate the story of the young prince who left his palace to seek truth and salvation in the midst of the poor, the old, and the sick. And many tales in the Bible could have satisfied the same need. But for some reason the designers of our school curriculum (several of whom, by the way, were my father's personal friends) chose not to use them, perhaps because, as secular humanists, they did not want to bring into the classroom anything that suggested institutional religion. Wilde's tale, not ostensibly religious but steeped in religion's flights of moral imagination, served their purpose well. It has left an indelible stamp on at least one child's mind—mine. After reading "The Happy Prince," I could never again confine the idea of "good" to merely fulfilling social obligations.

And so, in that little schoolhouse and under the constant threat of death by bombing, children were encouraged to reach for the sky. To develop our *human* potential to the fullest, we drew on the world's heritage. It now occurs to me that our teachers and parents were essentially indifferent to geography—to the colorful range of human livelihoods. Diversity in itself had little educational value if one culture was no better—that is, no more effective—than another at expanding the mind or extending human power. Our educators, though they might ardently espouse social equality, were elitists in learning. They took for granted that where one's achievements ranked mattered far more than where one happened to be located geographically in a mosaic of achievements, all deemed, a priori, to be of comparable worth.

The contrast with the American perspective can hardly be sharper. In the last quarter of the twentieth century, children in the United States have increasingly been encouraged to embrace their own traditions and, at the same time, consider cultural diversity as good in itself. Why is seldom made clear. Could it be by analogy with biological diversity? But why should biological diversity be considered good—good for what and for whom? For many people, the goodness of diversity, whether cultural or biological, is just common sense, and that idea may, in turn, have its source in such ordinary experiences as visits to the zoo, where it hardly requires arguing that the more kinds of animals there are the better, or to the ethnographic museum, the prestige of which is measured by the number and variety of dioramas, or to the shopping emporium, where having a wide range of goods matters more than having a few of outstanding quality.

Be that as it may, in the name of cultural diversity, I can envisage an America in which white children celebrate Thanksgiving, black children celebrate Kwanza; and if the trend continues, red children, brown children, and yellow children will all devote the better part of their energies celebrating their own harvest tradition. This understanding of culture, to the extent that it succeeds in implanting a strong sense of pride in the customs of one's group and a tolerance or fuzzy-minded approval of the customs of other groups, will achieve equality by making all young persons into ethnics or provincials, secure and content in their own corner of the world. What it misses is the potential in every young person to outgrow the hearth and become a cosmopolite, an individual free and able to pick the best wherever it occurs, and able—above all—to understand the underlying meaning and purpose of any cultural practice.[1]

As a child, I was conscious of being Chinese primarily because I was conscious of not being Japanese—and the Japanese loomed large because they had invaded our country. Isaac Newton? Benjamin Franklin? Their names were written in unusual Chinese characters in our textbooks. But I did not dwell on their non-Chineseness. I was far too engrossed in *what they did* to be interested in their national origin. They were just remarkable human beings I could admire and emulate. Young children pay hardly any attention to ethnic or racial differences. An African American child having fun with conic sections doesn't care whether a white man or a black man invented geometry. Children have to be told—as they are in some pride-building American schools—to admire first, if not only, heroes raised in their own hearth. Whatever the immediate gain of this approach, it is ultimately destructive of a young person's self-confidence as he or she moves onto the world stage.

A test of my own self-confidence came in 1941 when the Tuan family moved to Australia. My brothers and I, all younger than twelve, were enrolled in a school that was modeled after the British public school—a strange mix of young gentlemanly behavior and a "Tom Brown" ethos of male roughness. My brothers and I must have felt, at one level, totally out of place. We were the only Asians—not only then but in the entire history of the school (see fig. 1). We were puny, undernourished, compared with the robust Australians, and we didn't, at first, speak a word of English. In the first few months of school, we were subjected to almost relentless harassment. "Chin chien Chinaman, him very bad," the Australian boys chanted as they danced around us. Having read a famous story by Charles Lamb (1775–1834) in English class, they pretended to pull our nonexistent pigtails and pretended that we surfeited ourselves on an unending diet of roast pork.

So, what did my brothers and I do? Well, we did a most un-British thing: we tattled. First, we complained to our parents. A Chinese woman who overheard the complaint and who was herself not fluent in English told us to tell the bullies, "You are very rude. Nothing like that!" Ignorant as we were, we knew enough not to use that prissy rejoinder. We then informed our schoolmaster, who simply told us to fend for ourselves, unless the taunters made it physically difficult for us to attend class. And so we fought back, and we gave as good as we got, our righteous fury making up for our deficiencies in swear words and physical size. Soon, the ethnic slurs and harassment started to abate. At times, we enjoyed the fights so much that we quite forgot the offense to dignity that prompted them. My older brother happened to be athletic. That helped us to gain respect. We soon picked up English; from being dunces we began to do well academically, first in such subjects as math and physics, then in geography and history, and eventually in English itself.

I said earlier that, at one level, my brothers and I found ourselves in an

Fig. 1. The Tuan family in Sydney, 1943. My brothers and I are in our Cranbrook School uniforms.

alien and hostile environment. We felt out of place. But at a deeper level, we took for granted that we belonged in school—even in an Australian school (such was the success of Chinese indoctrination). The deep sense that we belonged made it possible for us to overlook even egregious signs of unwelcome. Attacks on Chinese customs and civilization had more power to annoy than to wound, for we had no sense of inferiority in these regards. They did, however, draw out an unfortunate streak of chauvinism that had entered our bloodstream despite inoculation with heavy doses of cosmopolitanism. My brothers and I concluded that people who guzzled milk and ate cheese—as these Australian boys did—were barbarians, like the unruly nomads beyond the Great Wall we read about in schoolbooks.

Confidence in Chinese civilization, I now call it. But couldn't it, after all, just be the confidence of class—a confidence that drew on myriad experiences of privilege? It never occurred to me, until recently, that I was raised in privilege. "Such obtuseness is typical of the bourgeoisie," a Marxist might say. My excuse, admittedly lame, is that in the rare times I wandered into the landscape of my Chinese childhood, I recognized poverty, and poverty just didn't mesh with my early understanding of what it meant to be privileged. We had so little in our last place of residence in China. We, a family of six, lived in a primitively furnished, three-room house. Our clothes—mother's and the children's—were homemade. True, Father wore custom-made suits, but he had to: his job at the foreign ministry required a minimum sartorial standard. We had barely enough to eat. Father occasionally brought home an apple or a banana, great delicacies that we cut into small slices and shared. He got them by bartering a tie or a handkerchief that some American friend gave him. The richest man in our village was the headmaster of Nankai Middle School. He—fabulously wealthy!—possessed a refrigerator. In long humid summers, he periodically distributed trays of ice cubes to his neighbors. One such tray arrived at our home while I was out watching a basketball game. My parents tried to save an ice cube for me. By the time I returned, there was just a thin wedge floating in a glass of water. I fished it out, tasted it, and was taken aback by its saltiness. Father labored under the impression that putting salt into the water would delay the melting.

Food was expensive and scarce. We suffered from undernourishment. My younger brother loved to eat and had an unusually big appetite. One day, when Father came home from work, my brother informed him with all the seriousness of a six-year-old that, henceforth, we could afford to eat only twice a day. This distressed Father so much that he decided to do everything he could to get himself transferred to a foreign country where he could feed his family properly, even if he had to accept substantial demotion, for many of his colleagues also wanted to escape. This was how we ended up in Australia in 1941.

In time, I learned that, even with severe material want, the perks of class and their subtle psychological boosts were there to fortify the self. Poverty bore no social stigma, because in war-ravaged China everyone who was not corrupt was poor. I should have wondered how we still enjoyed the services of two live-in servants: they were not paid, or were paid irregularly, because my father was paid irregularly. I should have taken greater notice of the educational level of my father and his friends. When they gathered to talk, as they often did in someone's living room, which was soon filled with cigarette smoke, or in the courtyard under bright stars in summer, the topics ranged casually from politics to astronomy, from Yuan dynasty drama to Russellian logic. And their Chinese was laced with English, French, and German words. And how could I have forgotten the paradox that, with hardly enough to eat ourselves, my parents nevertheless had the Honorable Nelson Johnson, the American ambassador, to dinner? Our humble home was turned inside out for that occasion. To create a dining room, which we didn't have, the furniture of our parents' bedroom was removed and stored in a neighbor's courtyard. We children were happily expelled. In a village that rarely saw an automobile, the ambassador's limousine, with tiny American flags fluttering over the mudguards, arrived like a glittering vessel from outer space.

I use words such as *citizen, civilization, world,* or *world stage* to suggest scope, power, and ambition. Chinese children in my school were encouraged to participate in an intellectual expansionism that reached far beyond national borders. They belonged to a worldwide network (*guanxi*) of the mind, such that any child could believe that he or she enjoyed a kissing-cousin relationship with the likes of Newton. I now wish to turn, or return, to expansionism and guanxi of a more sociopolitical kind.

As is well known, the higher the social class, the greater is the scale of its spatial and temporal operations. In China, families of the professional middle or scholar-gentry class were able to send their tentacles of influence well beyond the village, town, or clustering of towns in which they happened to reside. Family personalities and histories meshed with local, regional, and even national personalities and histories. Those of my family were no exception. As a child, I listened to Father's stories about our forebears and overheard (although I was not supposed to overhear) his gossip about bosses, colleagues, and other contemporaries. I did not know then that I was picking up knowledge about China and even, because China was a fair-sized player in the world, about the modern world. From such informal education at home and from formal lessons learned at school, I have come to identify myself far more with nation and national culture, and even with the world and world events, than with locality, whether this be my birthplace—Tianjin, which I had abandoned at age three to escape from the Japanese—or my hometown in Anhui province, about which I knew (and know) absolutely nothing.

Speaking this way—linking family to nation—sounds like boasting. And perhaps it is. But if so, it is only now that I can boast. In childhood and youth, I couldn't have taken special pride in the link between family and nation because I thought it was normal—true of everyone—and, in fact, it was true of nearly everyone I knew. America has so successfully branded me an ethnic that I have almost forgotten my citizenship in nation (Chinese or American) and in the world. How far this forgetting of my larger self has gone I realized a few years ago when I picked up a book called *The Chinese Century: A Photographic History of the Last Hundred Years* with the idea of refreshing my memory concerning the major historic events of modern China.[2] Our family story—my personal story—couldn't have been further from my mind. But as I looked at the pictures and read the texts, I was astonished by their air of familiarity.[3] Here, unexpectedly, is a picture of my forebear Tuan Ch'i-jui in the fancy uniform of a field marshal. He served as premier in the period 1912–1914 and was China's provisional president from 1924 to 1926. I heard a lot about him as a child. He was a patron of the Tuan clan. The Tuans were rooted in Anhui province. Long ago, perhaps during the T'ang dynasty (A.D. 618–907), they all huddled in one place and belonged to one extended family. Since then, the family split. By modern times, there were two major branches, one located in Yinshan (ours) and the other located in Hofei (Marshal/Premier/President Tuan's); one was poor (ours), the other rich. Marshal Tuan supported my father through school, with an interesting consequence that I shall soon relate. Meanwhile, let me note that the marshal's benign shadow followed me all the way to the United States. In 1956, in my first job interview at Indiana University, I was caught off guard when a professor of Asian history, who had a say in whether I was to be hired, exclaimed, "So you are the descendant of a president of China!" I thought he was joking until I recalled those stories from childhood. I got the job.

Another picture in *The Chinese Century* shows Wang Ching-wei in a tuxedo, toasting a German diplomat in 1940. And who was Wang Ching-wei? He was my mother's relative—a distant cousin. And what was my mother's relative doing in a history book published in the United States in 1996? Well, Wang was the Chinese Pétain. He collaborated with the Japanese while he served as premier from 1940 to 1944. He was the skeleton in the family closet. I remember hearing grown-ups talking about him with a mixture of anxiety and pride. Pride? Well, he was, after all, a national figure. In his own misguided way he was patriotic, for he thought that China could be saved only through collaboration with the overwhelming imperial force—Japan. As for anxiety, well, Wang Ching-wei was eventually denounced as a traitor by the Nationalist government under Chiang Kai-shek. My Nationalist parents sought to distance themselves from this relative—to disown him. And yet also to claim him. How not? The ties were too close. Wang became foreign minister in 1935, the year my father joined the foreign ministry. Surely there was a link there—guanxi? And this was not all: my mother's older brother served for a time, under Wang, as a vice minister of foreign affairs.

Let me return to Marshal Tuan. *The Chinese Century* was not very flattering in what it had to say about him. He was, apparently, your basic warlord, only more successful than most. I am prepared to overlook his faults because he did give my father financial support through Nankai Middle School. And that proved to be momentous, for at school my father's closest friend was Chou En-lai. They were, among other things, joint editors of the school magazine. And Chou's pictures, needless to say, are prominent in *The Chinese Century*, as they would be in any book on modern China—or even on modern world affairs. That "Uncle Chou" (as we children learned to call him) and Father could become close friends was surprising because Chou was a son of affluence and my father a son of genteel poverty. The rich boy became a Communist leader and an intimate colleague of Mao Tse-tung; the poor boy became a loyal follower of Chiang Kai-shek, whose passion was to destroy communism. Their political paths sharply diverged but their friendship held.

It held for several reasons. One was that, in the late 1930s, Nationalists and Communists were officially allies in their joint effort to combat the Japanese. Chou En-lai was stationed in the wartime capital. He came to our home from time to time. I remember him arm-wrestling with my father in the living room. Chou had hurt his arm in a fall, and Father was testing whether his friend's arm had regained its full strength. Another reason was sociophilosophical compatibility: both Chou and my father felt deep sympathy for the underdog, Chou through his idealism and Father through his experience as the poor boy as well as through idealism. Both were egalitarians. My father greatly admired the Soviet Union, as of course did Chou, for its championing of social justice. Father served as chef de protocol at the foreign ministry. One of his jobs was to escort newly accredited ambassadors up a mountain to the residence of the Chinese president, who was a dignified old gentleman by the name of Lin Seng. The only way up that mountain, other than walking, was on the backs of coolies, in sedan chairs. Ambassadors rode in sedan chairs as a matter of course, as did my father and other accompanying Chinese officials. But the Soviet ambassador refused. He insisted on walking, and so all the out-of-shape Chinese officials, including my father, had to huff and puff their way to the top. The result? The Soviet ambassador won my father's lasting admiration. There and then, my father decided to learn Russian. He sought to pass his new enthusiasm to his children by asking them to say *do svidaniya* (goodbye) every morning as he went to work.

Mao and Chou established the People's Republic of China in 1949. Chiang Kai-shek, with remnants of his government and army, moved to the island bastion of Taiwan. Henceforth, Chou En-lai and my father were in bitterly opposed camps. Officially enemies, privately they maintained fond memories of each other. In 1956 Father attended the International Labor Organization conference in Geneva on behalf of the Republic of China (Taiwan). Late one night in the hotel, just as he was about to turn in, there was a knock on the door. He opened it to find his younger brother, who had come all the way from Tianjin as Chou's emissary; his mission was to persuade Father to return to the mainland. He failed in his mission. Many years later, in 1973, my younger brother, San-Fu, met with Chou in the Great Hall of the People. They spoke of family matters for four hours— a rather heartwarming indication of how Chinese society could put personal and private needs above at least the routine affairs of state. Chou again invited Father to visit, arguing that because Father had retired, he could come as a private individual.

Note the unequal status of the two friends. Chou En-lai was the premier of China, a world figure; Father was merely an ambassador from a country (Taiwan) that was steadily losing international recognition. In trying to maintain a friendship across the lines of political enmity, Chou En-lai took all the initiative. He could because he was, after all, the boss. Father couldn't: had he tried, he would have been judged disloyal and dismissed. I say this to point out that though my immediate forebears were poor and though the positions Father occupied in the Chinese government hierarchy were middle level, through guanxi he and his family were nevertheless able to gain toeholds and purchases on the larger world.

Some of my front-seat glimpses into world events were quite accidental. Two occurred in 1946. Early that year, Father went to the Philippines as the Chinese consul general. Mother, my sister, and I joined him later, while my two brothers remained in a boarding school in Australia. The big event I

Fig. 2. Independence Day, July 4, 1946, Manila. My parents, in the fourth row up, sat next to two military officers. Mother is holding a fan.

witnessed was the formal granting of independence to the Philippines on July 4. After World War II, rarely a month went by without a newspaper headline's announcing the independence of yet another former colony. Independence ceremonies were flamboyant affairs: on the flickering screen of early television, one could see big white tents on carpet-like lawns, high officials decked in plumed helmets, their ladies attired in flowing gowns, their guards and servants in immaculate uniforms. This was history in capital letters. Almost all the independences were granted by European powers. Strange that the one I attended was granted by the American imperium. Under American auspices, the ceremony was rather relaxed. Almost anyone could find a seat close to the swearing-in stand in the open-air stadium (see fig. 2). Nevertheless, certain basic rules of protocol were followed. Thus the last person to make a grand entrance into the stadium was the American high commissioner, a former governor of Indiana, whose name, I believe, was Paul McNutt. He was still top dog. But after the ceremony, the first to leave was Manuel Roxas—the newly installed president of the republic.[4]

Later that year, Father was transferred to a post in London. So we all moved again. Airplanes were slow in those days. Getting to England required several overnight stops. The first was Calcutta, the second Karachi, the third Cairo, which was to be the last overnight stop before London. As our airplane flew over the Mediterranean Sea, it started to descend. The captain announced that we were going to land on the island of Malta, where we would be guests of the British government for the next three days. What happened? Well, the airplane following ours had developed engine trouble. Its passengers ordered an exchange: they would fly on in our airplane; we would get theirs. I was not amused. Malta's fabulous past had little appeal to an ignorant fifteen-year-old. Nor, at that age, did I appreciate witnessing history in the making, for personages no less than the viceroy of India, Lord Wavell, and the Indian leader Jawarhalal Nehru commandeered our airplane. They were on their way to London to finalize India's independence.

Just tagging along with Father could mean interesting encounters. But they did not seem to me so at the time. In a child's eyes, the Manila episode was little more than entertainment and the Malta episode an inconvenience. Only much later was I sufficiently worldly to make use of them as conversational gambits and for harmless name dropping. Direct benefits to my career, as a result of guanxi, came later. Let me mention two.

The first was my admission to Oxford University as an undergraduate in 1948. I couldn't have gotten in without the help of a family friend, a well-known Chinese playwright, who lived in Oxford and had influence with the university authorities. It is embarrassing for me to confess that I wasn't admitted the usual way. Only a special consideration of my background—what today in the United States would be called affirmative action—made it possible for me to be an Oxford man. To be fair to myself, I did take and pass the college-entrance examination papers like everyone else, with just one exception—the paper in classics, and classics meant either Latin or Greek. I knew neither, and no crash course could have remedied the deficiency in a field in which English schoolboys—my competitors—excelled. So the Chinese playwright, at my father's urging, went to bat for me. Or rather, he went to bat for the prestige of Chinese civilization. He managed to persuade Oxford, supposedly a bastion of immovable tradition, that classical Chinese should be considered a suitable substitute. So, here I was in the Examination School one warm summer day, translating the *Confucian Analects* while other candidates translated the *Aeneid* or the *Iliad*.

The second benefit, thanks to my father's intervention, came eleven years later, in 1959. I received a grant from the U.S. Office of Naval Research (ONR) to study the coastal landforms of Panama. Why Panama? One reason was purely scientific: the narrow Panamanian isthmus offered a unique opportunity to observe and compare two coasts that came under very different wave and tidal regimes. Another was strategic: in the 1950s the navy was exploring the possibility of a second water route across the isthmus, in case the existing one became incapacitated in a world war or reverted to Panamanian sovereignty. The third reason was the help (maps and transportation) that I could expect from the huge American navy base in Panama. The fourth reason was personal. The Taiwan passport I had at the time—I was still a long way from American citizenship—made it very difficult for me to travel, because fewer and fewer countries where I might do research accepted my passport. Panama was different. It recognized Taiwan rather than the People's Republic as China. My father, as the Chinese ambassador, could easily obtain a visa for me. I could also save ONR money by staying at the embassy.

My early efforts at studying the Pacific coast were frustrated by the lack of adequate transportation. Only a jeep could get me anywhere near the mangrove-covered shore. The navy personnel at the base refused to let me borrow a jeep even though I worked for ONR. I told Father my sad story. He said, "Let me see what I can do." I was reluctant to accept his help. After all, I was a grown man. But I acceded because I badly needed a jeep and my time in Panama was short. Father called the captain of the navy base and invited him and some of his officers to have dinner at the embassy. As liquor was passed around, Father pointed his cigar at me and said to the captain, "My son works for you, you know. He needs a jeep to do the job properly. Can you help?" "Of course, we can," replied the captain. "Just report tomorrow to the man in charge of the car pool."[5] Which I did. The man had heard from his superiors. He was about to issue me the jeep when he said, "But I can't legally do that, for I have to specify in what capacity you are employed at the base." He scratched his head while I waited tensely. He then wrote on my identification card, "Laundryman."

So every morning I picked up the jeep and (I liked to pretend to myself) the U.S. Navy's dirty underwear and went to the beach to do the washing. Of course, I did nothing of the sort. Often, in revising my résumé when applying for yet another grant, award, or honor, I have been tempted to slip in "laundryman" as one of my job qualifications. Only an uptight sense of honesty prevented me from doing so. I tell this story now to show, once again, that, given the confidence that comes naturally to people of a certain class, and especially given the actual experiences of privilege as my father's son, racial slurs and ethnic stereotyping—laundryman!—have no power to sting. They seldom occur, in any case. And when they do, I see them as ethnographic curiosities, sources of amusement, incidents that I might serve up during a conversational lull—or, for that matter, in my autobiography.

I call this chapter "World Stage and Public Events." I could have called it, "A Middle-Class Child's Toehold on the World." Under Father's big top of connections and influence, I made contacts, however brief and tangential, with significant happenings in China and elsewhere, and with personalities, Chinese and non-Chinese, of above-average charisma and power. As an adult and on my own, it was a different story. My world shrank to academia and to a small corner of it at that. My mental horizon continued to expand, but the people I knew were world figures only in the highly specialized fields in which they achieved distinction. They were not movers and shakers in the larger world, not really opinion makers or public intellectuals whose views regularly appeared in the popular media. Perhaps I ought to mention a few exceptions, for the record but also because they prove the rule.

Carl Ortwin Sauer was perhaps the most famous geographer-scholar I knew personally. His influence extended far beyond geography to the environmental movement and even to poetry, for his writing style was much admired by Charles Olson and other Black Mountain poets. Carl Sauer had a high opinion of himself, as he should, and yet he modestly said (sometime in the 1950s) that his being footnoted by Lewis Mumford was probably his best claim to immortality. Mumford was a towering cultural icon throughout the period of my young adulthood. I admired him without reservation. In 1972, greatly daring, I sent him a copy of my monograph for the Association of American Geographers, called "Man and Nature" as a tribute. I certainly didn't expect an acknowledgment of any kind. A week later, a package arrived from Armenia, New York. It was a book by Artur Glikson called *The Ecological Basis of Planning* (1971). Mumford was the editor. He inscribed it as follows: "To Yi-Fu Tuan, with warm respects, Lewis Mumford." Warm respects? I nearly fell out of my chair. Needless to say, I still have the book.

In 1975 I attended a conference in Washington, D.C., called "Children, Nature, and the Urban Environment." In one session, the biologist and noted author Paul Shepard and I were the principal speakers. Our commentator was no less a personage than Margaret Mead. She was then at the height of her fame, with a reputation that rested not only on her research but on her role as a public intellectual, addressing such momentous national issues as youth, education, and sex. Shepard and I were a bit wary, for Mead was reputed to be blunt. How did I fare? Well, she characterized my paper as "delicious." Delicious! And this from the no-nonsense "grandmother of the Western world."[6]

What about my own honors and awards? Haven't I become a notable

Fig. 3. Medalists of the American Geographical Society, The Explorers' Club, New York City, 1987. From left, James E. Vance Jr., Kenneth Hare, me, and Calvin F. Heusser. (Courtesy, American Geographical Society)

fish in the small pond of human geography? A pond is, of course, not the world, but even in that pond, during the 1980s and 1990s, I have shrunk rather than gained in size, so that—to academic geographers—I have become a minnow that, even when it flips about to attract attention, barely ruffles the water.

Yet I mustn't stop with this remark, for it gives a distorted impression. I *have* had a few successes—a few tokens of public recognition. For instance, every August I receive an invitation to attend a banquet of the American Chapter of Baker Street Irregulars in Chicago. Holmesiana is a recherché area of scholarship, and I am honored to be seen as a worthy contributor to it. And there is the distinction of appearing on the front page of the sports section of the *Sunday Times* of London. I have had that distinction too, courtesy of a cricketeer. A reporter asked him why he chose to read geography at Cambridge University. His answer was that he was converted to geography by accidentally coming across a book, written by a Chinese geographer, called *Topophilia*. In 1987 I received the Cullum Geographical Medal of the American Geographical Society (see fig. 3); a high honor, but I was especially tickled by the thought that the medal's first recipient was the explorer to the North Pole, Robert E. Peary. How the conception of merit changed in the discipline of geography! From recognizing someone for his physical stamina, technical prowess, and dedication to a well-defined geographical goal to recognizing someone for his quasi-literary, quasi-philosophical probes into the murky worlds of value and emotion. Last, I must mention the Haskins Lecture, "A Life of Learning," which I gave in the Benjamin Franklin Hall, Philadelphia, in the year of my retirement (1998) at the invitation of the American Council of Learned Societies. Now, the ACLS is no small pond. By any reasonable reckoning, it is "the world." So what does that do to my claim of marginality—to my partly self-inflicted, partly involuntary isolation? Well, without ungraciously detracting from the effort of friends who obtained the invitation for me, I am convinced that fluke also played a major role. We academics too easily forget that unearned honor—honor that comes to us by a chance conflation of forces—happens quite as often as unearned neglect.

Public life has never seemed quite real to me—least of all the social functions that went with it. I thoroughly disliked them when Father, after my mother's death, insisted that I participate as cohost. At cocktail parties, official dinners, during national celebrations, the emptiness of the conversation beneath the multilingual sparkle, the play of power, the struggle for status under the cover of politesse, appalled and bored me (see fig. 4). As a mature adult, I took part in public events of the sort that were duly re-

Fig. 4. Cocktail party at the Chinese Embassy, Panama City, 1959. Father and I were the only ones in suits. The small talk didn't appeal to me.

ported to the departmental chair and passed on to the college dean. When I began planning for my autobiography, I thought that these accounts of accomplishments would come in handy. They rarely did, except as a reminder of what I was thinking about at different stages of my career. Contributing to public events—giving lectures, attending conferences, and serving on evaluation committees in different cities, and so on—does reflect a facet of my personality but one that is superficial and of no interest to anyone, not even me. By contrast, when I relate private and personal matters, as I do in the next two chapters, I feel, paradoxically, that I am at last saying something centrally human and widely shareable and thus of an import beyond the vain and boastful self.

3

Personal: From Parents to Stone

I N TELLING the more personal side of my story, I will use the family
album as a model, with some important departures. A family album
typically contains pictures of parents, oneself, and one's siblings when
young, and then the successive stages of maturation—birthday parties,
school graduations, weddings, anniversaries, and so on—chronologically
arranged. What I offer in this chapter resembles the family album in that I
begin with my parents, and I introduce "pictures" of the past in a roughly
chronological order. Also resembling it is the absence of bridges between
the pictures. No one expects complete coverage in a family album. Using it
as a model therefore allows me to be highly selective and excuses me from
the onerous task of filling in the blanks. Moreover, following its format
promises an end product that will have at least the appeal of simplicity.

But the model also suffers a serious disadvantage, for, given my antipa-
thy toward familial and social rites, most pictures in my album are irrele-
vant to my sense of self (see fig. 5). Far from revealing who I am, they can be
a distraction from, even a cover-up of, my real self, which, if it occurs
anywhere, lies buried in just those gray patches between the pictures. Although I am ready to acknowledge that psychoanalytic digging among
them can uncover certain crucial experiences and events, I choose not to
follow that path. Lack of technical competence is an obvious reason, but a
stronger reason is that I find another path—one that poets favor—both
more revealing and more congenial. Will this second path be justified by
the truths that it, and it alone, can reveal? Or am I just following it out of
laziness and self-indulgence? The experimentation that is this autobiography will produce the answer.

Fig. 5. My acute sense of self at an early age. The picture shows all the cousins who happened to be in Shanghai in 1938. I am the little boy at the extreme lower right who refused to hold his cousin's hand, preferring to hold his own.

A radical difference in the philosophy and procedure of the two paths is this: whereas psychoanalysts have to dig hard and long for their images, which are valued for their "truth content" almost in the measure that they are murky and strange, poets do not dig. Poets wait for their images to emerge or to make a sudden impression on their conscious awareness; these images, contrary to those sought in psychoanalysis, are often—or often appear to be—the commonplaces of life. The question then is why do just *these* images—these commonplaces—emerge? "Why," to quote T. S. Eliot, "for all of us, out of all that we have heard, seen, felt, in a lifetime, do . . . [the song of one bird, the leap of one fish, an old woman on a German mountain path] recur, charged with emotion, rather than others?"[1] What do such vivid impressions (and they are not all visual) signify? What do they reveal of a life—a self ?

I begin with my parents, and I do so somewhat reluctantly, for not only does such a start seem pedestrian but it is too deterministic: it puts too much weight on genes and early conditioning in the making of a human individual. But there is no avoiding the pervasive and penetrating influence of parents. The very shape and constitution of my body are a reminder of

34

my limited power to escape the parental template. Sharing as I do Nicholas Berdyaev's dislike of family resemblance, I am nevertheless forced to confront it every time I look into the mirror: up to a certain age, I had my mother's features; beyond, and increasingly, those of my father. Fortunately, I am more my own person in mental characteristics, though even there I see a resemblance, especially in my weaknesses.

I was much closer to my mother than to my father. Yet the memories that haunt me are mostly those in which my father figures prominently. Many are either unhappy or ambivalent. Perhaps that explains the difference: happiness—ordinary happiness as distinct from ecstatic joy—leaves no trace.

My father was a conscientious parent who modeled his behavior after an ideal that he had picked up in the United States. He wanted to distance himself from his own father's coolness and harshness, the patriarchal posture esteemed in old China. I admired and respected my father for having done his best. What more could a son ask? Well, unreasonably and unfilially, I could ask that he tried less hard. The irony is that less would have been more. Whereas the traditional Chinese father often acted against his natural inclination, pretending coolness when he was fond, repelling with formality when he wished to hug, my own idealistic father strained in the opposite direction. The care he showed us seemed to me to derive more from an adherence to principle than from a natural upwelling of affection. When we were sick, Father bought us toys. He had learned that it was the proper thing to do. As a child, I certainly appreciated the toys. I played with them; they distracted me. At the same time, with paint boxes and miniature trucks piling a little higher each day I spent in bed, I felt under mounting pressure to recover quickly and return to where I belonged—school. What I needed but did not get was reassurance that I really was sick, that no truly caring adult would suspect me of being a truant.

I have another memory that I wish to erase and can't. In our early teens, my brothers and I read the Sunday comics in bed until nine or later in the morning. We didn't see the indulgence as especially reprehensible, perhaps because we were growing up fast and needed the extra rest. Recent research shows that teenagers require something like ten hours of sleep a day. Father, of course, couldn't have known this. Had he known, I believe he would still have disapproved. He showed his disapproval by checking our bedroom periodically, each time with greater irritation. Finally, he stood at the door and cracked his knuckles. But it was how he looked that disturbed me most—the look of distaste. I have never had children of my own. I can imagine myself looking at them in anger. But in distaste?

Father lacked the ability to put himself in another's shoes. He was naively egotistical. His needs came first. Having gotten up, dressed, and ready for work or play, he couldn't understand why his children might want to loll about. Let me give one more example from a later decade, even if my remembrance of it exposes my own pettiness. As an adult, I visited Father in his various diplomatic posts abroad. After Mother's death, I shared his bedroom in the embassy at his insistence. One trivial inconsideration that I can't get out of my mind is that he invariably switched on the ceiling light when he wanted to go to the bathroom or just to know the time. That he could have done both without the gala illumination that was sure to shock me to wakefulness never occurred to him.

Not all fathers, I have come to realize, are so disregarding of their children's personalities and needs. A Wisconsin friend of mine offers a striking counterexample. In 1992 he flew out to the east coast to help celebrate his father's eightieth birthday. He was accompanied by his fifteen-year-old son. My friend's father kept alarm clocks in various parts of the house, all set to go off at seven in the morning. They all did go off the next morning. My friend told me how he rushed frantically from room to room, trying to locate the clocks and stop the alarm before it succeeded in waking his boy, who (he felt) needed the extra sleep. What a dad! I listened in envy. I was envious of his son but even more of him, for how could his son not respond in gratitude and affection—if not in overt ways now, then ten or twenty years later?

One of the joys of life is to walk into a room and see genuine welcome— a flush of happiness—on another's face. In childhood, parents, more than others, provide that welcome. The warmth of their smiles makes their children feel wanted, gives them the confidence and strength to negotiate the indifference and hostility of the world outside. When we lived in Sydney, Mother took us shopping from time to time to refurbish our school wardrobes. We went downtown in a trolley car. This outing was considered a treat, for we always stopped somewhere for afternoon tea and cakes. At the end of the day, we dropped by Father's office with our packages to hitch a ride home. Did Father ever break into a smile upon seeing us? Surely he must have done so. But—cursed memory!—I can only recall absentminded acknowledgment and even annoyance.

I now understand why. Father's job in Sydney was not an easy one. As chief consular officer, he had to deal with not only office politics, made petty by isolation in a foreign land, but also the flood of intractable problems of his motley constituency of Chinese laborers and workers, merchant sailors and store clerks, small traders and big businessmen. He never cared much for the consular job, which frustrated his desire for high-level diplomacy in a civilized, multilingual setting. He was not able to forget that, for his family's sake, he had had to accept a substantial demotion. Only by making a career sacrifice was he permitted to take his family out of food-scarce China for cornucopian Australia.

Still, our encounters in his office could have been more genial. Father just might have mustered sufficient warmth to meet his children's natural ebullience halfway. I know this is possible, for I have recently read an instance of it in a biography of Malcolm Muggeridge. Maybe it is unfair to compare my father with Muggeridge's father, for their situations and responsibilities differed markedly. But, fair or not, I will make it. When Muggeridge was old enough, he often traveled to London to spend part of the day with his father. He walked up to his father's office. And this is what Muggeridge wrote much later. "When he saw me, his face always lit up, . . . thereby completely altering his appearance; transforming him from a rather cavernous, shrunken man into someone boyish and ardent. He would leap agilely off his stool, wave gaily to his colleagues . . . and we would make off together."[2]

Of course, I also have fond memories of life with Father. One of the earliest was when I was about seven and lost my shoes in the mud. He carried me piggyback through the town to shop for a new pair—just the two of us. And there was the incident that I mentioned earlier, of my father's heroic but ineffectual effort to save an ice cube for me. Another memory, from a later period, sees me a fifteen-year-old student at La Salle College—an American Catholic school—in Manila. The classes, especially math, provided more challenge than I could handle. One hot mosquito-infested night, I struggled without success to solve a problem in binomial theorem. Father tried but could not help. I wept in frustration and from a profound sense of inadequacy. Instead of being angry, as I fully expected him to be, he shared my mortification and vowed to find a tutor for me.

My most sharply etched memory of Father is, unfortunately, a childhood nightmare. I must have been eight or nine. We lived, as I mentioned earlier, in a village outside Chongqing. My brothers and I made a habit of walking down a tree-lined road to meet Father at the bus stop. I remember it as a happy occasion. We were young enough that even a lumbering bus from the city exuded a certain glamor. As people came out of the bus, we searched for Father's face—and there he was! We rushed forward to greet him. In my nightmare, I walked alone down the tree-lined road. It was almost evening. Fog had rolled in. I felt uneasy, as one would when a familiar landscape assumes a strange mien. At that moment, I saw Father at a distance. He was moving toward me. So the bus had arrived early. I ran to meet him. Now I could see him, now I couldn't, because of the swirling fog. Each time I saw him, he was a little nearer and bigger in size. He disappeared. Then, suddenly, he was right before me. In relief (for I was feeling very scared), I opened my arms wide to hug . . . what? An apparition stood there, recognizably my father but draped in burial clothes, and it shifted about in the changing currents of air as though it had no weight. It was a ghoul—a corpse, with yellow unseeing eyes.

Children have nightmares from time to time. They wake up in sweat and dare not return to sleep. But with the coming of daylight the horror evaporates as though it never existed. That was how it was with me, except for the nightmare I have just recounted. I went through the next school day fairly well, but as night approached I began to feel anxious. A favorite older cousin of ours was visiting. I told her about my nightmare. One might think that the act of repeating it to a sympathetic ear would reassure me. Instead, the horror returned in full force. Even now, as I relate this dream of sixty years ago, I feel a slight chill in the air.

Father died in Taipei in 1980. He was in intensive care for two weeks. I could have flown out to be with him, as my two brothers did. While he lived, I was the son who sought his company; I was the one who visited him at his various foreign posts. Yet when he lay dying, I chose not to go. No doubt there were reasons for this shocking dereliction of filial duty, some of which I could not then, nor can I even now, understand. At the time I did see two reasons clearly. One was my abomination of the Chinese attitude toward death as embodied in its funeral practices. My distaste probably has its source in the village funerals that frightened me as a child—the rooster ever ready to herald the resurrection of the dead. I could not stomach the superstition of a bygone era or the dusty rites of filial piety that could only falsify sentiment. The second reason, as I have made abundantly clear, was my conflicted feelings toward Father. To pile them atop the bathos and falsities of the Chinese funeral—to me, a severe indictment of Chinese civilization—would have been more than I, never much endowed with either physical or moral stamina, could bear.

I loved Mother. But demandingly. As a child I demanded love from Mother all the more because I knew, quite early, that I couldn't expect it from Father. Father was open about his favorites: they were his first born and his third born. Favoritism toward number one son is traditional in China. As for favoritism toward the third son, well, Father himself was third in birth order, and that, apparently, was reason enough. Number two—me!—was just out of luck (see fig. 6). Even worse was to be born a girl. My sister, the youngest child, instead of being my parents' darling, as she would have been in an American family, was treated—not badly for

Fig. 6. This is the earliest picture of me—six months old? I am the bald one. Shaving the head was a Chinese custom. Supposedly it helped to maintain one's hair into old age. It didn't work! My brother Tai-Fu has his arm around me. Taken in 1931, Tianjin.

that would have offended one of my father's strongly held principles—but dutifully, with at times barely suppressed irritation.

Mother, it seemed to me as a child, did not have strong favorites. I campaigned hard to be one. How hard, I realized only in adulthood when I looked at the family album and found that I was nearly always posed next to her, pushing aside my younger brother, who as the youngest boy had the right to be there (see fig. 7). One of my most vivid early memories is of Mother drawing a motorcar. I can see the motorcar even now, its boxy form, its twin cone-shaped lamps, its big wheels protected by arched half-moon mudguards. I was about four and already had fixed ideas on the roles my mother could play. Artistic endeavor wasn't one of them. I asked her what the picture was for. She replied that she drew it to amuse my younger brother, who was then taking his afternoon nap.

Mother was mildly tubercular during her childbearing years, so she did not nurse us. In any case, the custom in those days was for the lady of the house to turn this basic maternal function over to someone else. Father, enlightened by his exposure to Western values, objected to the practice, for it meant that a country woman had to abandon her own newborn (almost always a girl) to nurture another woman's child. Nonetheless, Father hired

Fig. 7. Seeking to displace my younger brother in my mother's affection. I am immediately next to my mother, leaning slightly against her, where my younger brother should be (he is the boy at far right). The picture was taken in 1940 or early 1941, in Chongqing, as we were preparing to leave for Australia.

wet nurses, with the result that in our earliest years our most intimate contacts were with a stranger. She took care of most day-to-day things. My own nurse not only gave me her milk, wiped my nose, and scolded me for naughtiness but also (though illiterate herself) encouraged me, by the time I was a toddler, to learn Chinese characters. As a result, Mother became a rather distant, dignified, and glamorous figure, someone who, unlike the nurse, invariably smelled nice.

At age seven, I discovered aspects of my mother that I had not known before—an all-enveloping tenderness toward her young when they needed it and a surprising fierceness toward the external world when it appeared to be threatening. To give the reader an idea of these qualities, I need to open up my canvas and tell the story of our escape from the invading Japanese army. We were always on the move, staying in this city for one year, that city for two years, but sooner or later the Japanese were again dogging our heels. Our last dramatic flight was to China's last stronghold—Chongqing. We took two big leaps, one by sea from Shanghai to Haiphong (Hanoi's port city) and the other by land from Hanoi to Kunming and thence to Chongqing.

In the summer of 1938, Father left Nanjing with other foreign ministry people for the wartime capital of Chongqing. His family was to follow later, which we did. For the first time, Mother was in sole charge of four young children. We piled into an antiquated bus. Our route was the famous (or notorious) Burma Road, built hastily over some of the world's most rugged terrain to provide a lifeline for besieged China. The road made innumerable hairpin bends; it seldom had guard rails, often sloped the wrong way, and its surface was either washboard or full of holes. With distressing frequency, it washed out, which meant that our bus and a whole convoy of vehicles would have to wait many hours, a whole day, or even longer. Rain and fog were frequent, as were accidents. From time to time, we were told that a bus ahead of us had plunged into a gorge or that two buses had collided. Corpses and survivors wrapped in blood-stained bandages lined the road, again making it impossible for us to pass. One day—I remember this clearly—our bus climbed higher and higher up a mountain. Light rain and mist made it difficult for the driver to see. At the worst possible moment, the windshield wiper stopped working and, at the same time, a baby started to cry. The driver (whom we called "Engineer," a more prestigious title) stopped the bus and said, "Throw out the baby! Either the baby or we will all die!" The passengers pleaded with the engineer, passed the baby to the back of the bus, and tried to smother his cries with clothes and blankets. (Although I've never been sure, I think they succeeded in keeping the baby quiet enough to placate the driver.)

We children at first took the journey for a lark. After a couple of days on the road, during which we were forced to endure long hours of confinement and boredom interrupted by sudden threats to life, our mood changed: we became more and more irritable and restless. Mothers had to find ways to distract their broods, making sure that they did not annoy the increasingly bad-tempered and autocratic driver. I presented a special challenge, for I suffered from a painful skin disease—probably a consequence of malnutrition. Periodically, my entire body broke out in rashes, which within a few hours turned into pearl-colored boils filled with pus. Mother lanced them with her sewing needle, applied ointment, and wrapped nearly my entire body in gauze. Thoroughly miserable, I whined, fussed, and made endless demands. So it was on the Burma Road that I tested a quality in Mother that I had not known before—tenderness and inexhaustible patience.

At last we were at the outskirts of Chongqing. Through the darkness and rain, we could see city lights flickering in the distance. There was one more bridge to cross. Father, we learned later, was waiting for us at the other end. Then came the bad news that our bus was too heavy to cross the bridge, which had been weakened by flood. The bridge was being repaired, but each time the repair work was about to be completed, it was undone by private cars driven fast and recklessly over it. So, once again, we had to wait. But for how long? In the end, we decided to walk. Mother got us ready. Outside the bus, porters from the city swarmed around the passengers, bidding to carry the luggage. It was a nightmare of confusion—disoriented men and women, crying children, shouting porters, suitcases and trunks all over the place. As soon as I stepped off the bus, I lost both shoes to the sticky mud. The gauze around my legs came loose. I was soaked by the rain and refused to walk another step. Mother was carrying my sister and couldn't carry me too. My older brother, only eight years old, was strong and remarkably independent, but my younger brother clearly needed attention. That was when Mother, to my surprise, grabbed a porter by the arm and ordered him—in a voice so commanding that it brooked no refusal—to drop the trunk he was carrying and carry me instead. He obeyed instantly. The trunk, packed with—who knows?—silk and fur? (it obviously belonged to a rich man), was dumped and I rode high on the porter's back.

By the time I entered my midteens, the feeling I had for Mother was not only fond but increasingly protective. In being protective, I might simply have assumed a role expected of a male child. Mother, I knew, didn't need my help: she valued her independence and could be formidable when the occasion demanded it. Nevertheless, my overall impression of her was one of vulnerability. She seemed to me too unworldly and this despite her dutiful participation in my father's world of diplomacy, politics, and status aspiration. Unlike Father, Mother preferred to be out of the limelight. She enjoyed the simple things of life, such as buying clothes and shoes for her children, stopping by a shop for afternoon tea (a habit she picked up in Westernized Shanghai and continued in Australia, England, and France), and buying a Christmas tree and its trinkets, even though celebrating Christmas wasn't really our custom. She made it our custom because it generated a mix of warmth and playfulness that she liked. Nothing she did was ostentatious, certainly not the things she bought, and that included the Christmas tree, which stood barely five feet tall.

Years later (in 1956), Father was appointed ambassador to Panama. My parents decided to come over to the United States and visit me and my brothers before taking up the new post. I was in my first job, at Indiana University. I bought an old Hudson from a colleague for three hundred dollars and drove it to New York to meet my parents. The entire family checked into a Manhattan hotel. Our parents' unit had a small kitchen. Late at night, when we were hungry again after all the talking and laughing, Mother would cook us a delicious supper of noodles. We were happy—happy in an innocent, sunny, cloudless way that I couldn't recall our ever having known before. Father soon left for Panama. Mother, however, decided to stay longer in the United States—in California, where San-Fu, my younger brother, was completing his Ph.D.—and, for that matter, so was I, for I took the Indiana job without the degree in hand. So we drove out to California in my old clunker. On the long trip west, Mother seemed to me like a child in her appreciation of new experience. Her only complaint was a persistent backache, which she attributed to riding in a car for long hours. That backache turned out to be the early symptoms of the pancreatic cancer that would kill her a few months later.

Our temporary California home was a handsome house in the Berkeley hills. Mother loved it, but she was afraid to stay there alone. So she came down with us to the campus every day and spent time shopping, sitting on a bench watching the busy student life around her, enjoying the fragrance of the sun-baked eucalyptus trees—a fragrance she recalled from our years in Australia—and socializing with a newfound American friend, the mother of one of my classmates. One night, fairly late, I had to return to the university to draft some maps in the cartographic lab. Mother came with me. The idea was that my younger brother would pick her up at the parking lot next to Giannini Hall, where I was to work. We waited a while. Mother then persuaded me to go in. She would wait alone. Three hours later, I returned to the car, opened the door, and found Mother curled up on the front seat, asleep. There had been a misunderstanding. My brother had never appeared. I was shocked, for even in the 1950s the campus could be dangerous after dark. But Mother didn't seem to mind—or, rather, she was so relieved to see me that she forgot whatever anxiety she might have felt. Her anxiety, in any case, was not driven by realistic threats. She just wanted to be near someone she knew. My being in a building a few steps away consoled her, even though she couldn't get to me, for the building was locked at night.

This experience forcefully impressed on me that our roles had reversed and that it was up to us children, now in our twenties, to take care of Mother. She was only fifty-five, but sickness—how sick none of us knew at the time—had sapped her energy and self-confidence. When the back pain momentarily eased, she could still be lively and happy, playing Ping-Pong under the porch of our rented house, experimenting with food in her splendid American kitchen, going down to Shattuck Avenue for family rites of tea and cake, doing the sorts of things she always enjoyed. Other times, she could look distracted, bewildered, and a little scared.

So the days passed. As September approached, Mother and I both grew uneasy, although neither of us said anything. Soon I would have to drive back to Indiana to teach. The fateful day came. I got up early and so did Mother. We went into town for a leisurely breakfast—a delaying tactic Mother invented. Finally, I said I had to go. But Mother had another trick up her sleeve. She insisted that I be supplied with California oranges for my long drive east. She would come with me to the supermarket. At the super-market, I waited with my brother and sister at the checkout counter while Mother walked down the aisle, picking out the oranges. She took her time. Finally, she came toward us with an armful. We walked out to the car, and I opened the door and put in the oranges. I turned to say good-bye. She embraced me, a gesture she seldom made (it was not the Chinese custom), and wept.

Mother joined Father in Panama. Soon after, she was hospitalized. When the local doctors announced that the disease was cancer, Father flew Mother up to Columbia-Presbyterian Medical Center in Manhattan for treatment. An exploratory operation showed that the cancer was too advanced to be removed or cured. As Mother returned to consciousness after the operation, she looked at her family gathered around her bed. We smiled encouragement, which she immediately took to be good news: she thought she would recover. None of us had the heart to tell her otherwise. We waited day after day, helplessly, as she steadily declined. The hospital waiting room became for me a surreal place of disembodied voices, footsteps, light and shadow on the wall changing pattern as the sun moved across the sky, pasty-faced humans occupying padded chairs that were incongruously cheerful, like those in a summer resort. My body felt leaden. I dragged it from place to place. But my mind was curiously light, emptied by fatigue and hopelessness. One day, around three in the morning, when we were all dozing, a nurse came to announce that Mother was near her end and would we please go to her. I struggled out of my chair and smoothed out my rumpled coat. One button was missing. I looked for it under the cushion and under the chair and wondered stupidly whether it could have rolled into the heating duct.

My album contains pictures of not only kin but friends. Let me now turn to one of them. Friendship, to occur, must satisfy the two basic requirements of common interest and warm, mutual liking. In an ideal friendship, the two requirements should be in some sort of balance, for tipped too much in the direction of common interest, the pair are more colleagues than friends; tipped too much in the other direction, they may find themselves lovers, looking into each other's eyes rather than at the world. I cannot risk falling in love, for reasons that will become clear in the next chapter. My friendships therefore rest on common interest. But it too has its risks. For if the common interest is human nature and condition, the sympathies and antipathies of the friends may (and, I would even say, should) be engaged. Without the engagement, their shared pursuit can only be superficial. With the engagement—with the kind of prolonged discussion of feelings and mental states that draws on personal as well as impersonal experience— the emotional temperature between friends is almost sure to rise. To avoid such a path, its inconveniences and dangers, the friends can always concentrate on the inorganic world—on physical geography, or on the human world in a cool, quasi-statistical way.

I realize that what I have just said sounds grim—as though life and its emotions are a temptation to be kept at a safe distance. It is grim. But not as grim as one might think, for the pursuit of knowledge itself can be passionate, all the more so if it is done in the company of a genial, equally committed friend.

Let me tell the story of my friendship with David Harris in the years between 1954 and 1963. In the winter of 1954, I was in southeastern Arizona, doing fieldwork for my doctoral dissertation on a special kind of desert landform called a pediment (see fig. 8). I made my headquarters in a ramshackle boardinghouse in Tucson. From there I went into the field, where I stayed for periods of three to five days. I enjoyed my time in the field. The semiarid landscape is austerely beautiful, the temperature just right—warm during the day, cool after sunset. A great deal of my pleasure must be attributed to the rapid progress I was making in my pediment study. I knew what to map—what sort of evidence to look for. By around five o'clock, I would stop working. I was too physically exhausted to do more. I would cook a meal with canned food on my Coleman stove. I had converted my 1940 Ford two-seater into a bed by putting an orange crate next to the steering wheel and lifting the back of the seat to expose a hole that led into the trunk. I could lie flat in the Ford with my head resting on the crate, my back supported by the seat, and my legs thrust into the trunk. I hung a lamp on the rearview mirror and read by it as I lay stretched out on my makeshift bed. Soon the words on the page would blur and I would fall asleep.

It was not a bad routine, except for two things. One was that my car was not equipped to negotiate the rough and often trackless terrain of the desert. Periodically, it sank into the sand. Neither strong nor apt, I was never confident that I could free it. As the hours slipped by and I had made no perceptible progress, my mounting frustration, tinged with fear, would make me even less competent. The second problem was that I did not know

Fig. 8. A pediment is the entire bedrock surface at the foot of a mountain range; this one is in southeastern Arizona. I took this picture in 1954.

how to occupy myself at the end of the day. After the evening meal, the sun was still up. I could hardly go to bed, but I was too tired to do anything else—even to read.

All this changed when David Harris, a student from England, joined me. David went from Oxford to Berkeley on a George V fellowship. We missed each other at Oxford; by the time he came up, I had left for California. We missed each other again at Berkeley; he arrived after my departure for the Arizona desert. We were strangers but had many experiences and intellectual interests in common. Our rapport was immediate. Out in the field, my little car sank again and again into the sand. Its wheels spun to no effect. Rather than experiencing frustration or despair, as I had in the past, I was surprised to find myself actually enjoying the challenge of freeing the car. David's presence made all the difference. I was comforted by his practi-

cality, cheered by his cheerfulness. Above all, he had patience and fortitude, qualities I singularly lacked and therefore admired all the more.

Let me illustrate. Before David arrived, I took an extended trip into a
remote part of southeastern Arizona. I walked for hours, climbing up and
down gullies and massive boulders to reach an armchair-shaped bedrock
surface—an unusually convincing example of a pediment. I mapped its
outer edge, which was defined by a fault line, and took many pictures,
which were to provide visual evidence for my thesis of how it came into
being.

A week or so later, David arrived. We drove back into the desert and
stopped for lunch under the only shade we could find. It occurred to me
that I should remove the film that contained the crucial pictures from my
last outing and install a new roll in preparation for the next stage of our
work. The camera's knob refused to turn. The film was jammed. I would
have to open the camera to retrieve it. But to do so I needed to find a place
of total darkness. The only totally dark place in that bright landscape was
the inside of a sleeping bag. So I dived into my sleeping bag, zipped it shut
to prevent any light from penetrating by chance, and tried to free the film.
A minute passed, then two, then three, then four. It seemed to me an eter-
nity. I was sweating profusely. I couldn't breathe. I came out to admit failure. I lamented to David that I would have to return to the pediment. David
offered to try. He dived into my sleeping bag. One minute, two minutes . . .
five minutes. I could see the bag going through contortions like a boa con-
strictor that had swallowed a protesting rabbit. I shouted to David to come
out. He either didn't hear me or chose to ignore me. Six minutes, seven
minutes . . . ten minutes! "David, for God's sake, come out before you
suffocate!" He came out triumphant, with the freed roll of film in his hand.
Full of admiration, I told him: "I now know how the British Empire was
won."

One day, after many hours of mapping, we quit work to set up camp at
the top of an immense alluvial fan. From there we could see miles of desert
and no obvious human imprint. "Camp" did not mean anything elaborate.
I was going to sleep in my car, as I always had. David had said that he
would enjoy sleeping under the cloudless night sky. For supper I warmed
up two cans of Irish stew; not exactly cuisine, but to famished geographers
it was fit for the gods. I boiled water and made coffee. We drank it. My
watch registered seven o'clock. The sun had not yet set, and it was obviously far too early to turn in. What to do? David said that we should enjoy
the desert air in style. I wasn't sure what he had in mind but followed his
instruction to pull the seat out of the car. We did this easily enough, for
almost everything in my old Ford could be detached if given a sufficient

tug. We dragged the seat some distance and placed it on the alluvial fan. David produced, to my surprise, a bottle of sherry and two elegant wine glasses. The seat, nondescript and wholly ignorable in the car, looked orphaned and touchingly civilized in the vast bleak space of the desert. We sat on the padded seat and touched our glasses. "To the Queen!" I said.

Darkness eventually covered the land. The wind that had buffeted my eardrums all day had died down. I became aware of a silence that, though soothing at first, grew into an immense and increasingly oppressive presence as the minutes passed. I thought of breaking the silence by telling David a ghost story that I had heard long ago in China. Why a ghost story? Well, for one thing, a ghost town lay nearby. Though we couldn't see it from our camp, I knew it was there, for I had explored its abandoned stores and homes on an earlier occasion. I had had the eerie feeling then that, at any moment, I might bump into the ghost of a miner coming down the street, or even a Chinese laundryman in his little store, which stood remarkably intact. As to why I chose this particular ghost story from the many I knew, the answer lay deeper. It had to do, I now believe, with my deepening friendship with David. Yoked genially to him around the clock made that inevitable. The relationship gave me satisfaction but also aroused unease, as almost all human relationships beyond the superficial did. Why? What was my problem? The ghost story itself suggests an answer. This is what I said, more or less.

Two school friends, Wang and Wei, grew up together and were inseparable. One summer, they made plans to spend their holidays exploring the limestone caves of the Purple Mountains. These were within sight of their school in clear weather and could be reached in a good day's walk. They started early. Somewhere along the way they must have made a wrong turn, for by nightfall they were still nowhere near their destination. Instead, they found themselves in a bewildering landscape of hills and valleys. Darkness made further travel foolish. They looked for a place to camp and eventually settled for a sheltered hollow. Wei would have preferred to search further. He was averse to the hollow but couldn't make himself say why, which was that burial mounds in various stages of decay and abandonment ringed the site.

Wang was one of those who could sleep on his feet if necessary. In no time at all, Wei heard his friend snoring. Wei, however, could not sleep. He tossed on the ground and estimated the passing of the hours by noting how far the moon had risen. He felt an urge to relieve himself. Because the night had turned cold, getting up required an act of will. He walked a few steps, or what seemed to him just a few steps, out of sight of the camp and did his business. More comfortable now, he was sure that sleep would overtake him as soon as he snuggled back into his blankets. He smiled in anticipation. He turned around a hill, expecting to see the camp. But there was no camp. He turned around another hill, then another, and another, with mounting anxiety. He could, of course, call. Wang must still be within hearing distance. Yet he did not call, for what if someone else answered?

Wei stopped rushing about. He realized that he was quite lost and so had no reason to move in one direction rather than another. He tried to breathe slowly and evenly, to get a grip on himself. There was no cause for panic yet. He stood still and looked around. He saw a light blinking in the distance. It would not take him to where he wanted to go, but anything was better than paralysis. He ran toward the light, losing it with each dip in the ground, finding it again with the next rise. At last, he came to an abandoned farmhouse. All the rooms were dark except one. Wei walked to the one lit window and looked in. He could make out an old woman sitting on a stool with her back toward him. She was combing her long white hair before a mirror. Her movements were awkward. She had trouble reaching to the back of her head. She sighed a deep sigh, raised her arms to her head, and took it off and placed it before her so that she could comb more easily.

Wei froze. His hands felt glued to the window sill, his feet soldered to the ground. With a violent jerk he tore himself free. He ran as fast as he could. The hills made running difficult, for while his feet beat on firm ground going upslope, they trod disconcertingly on nothing but air on the way down. He fell, picked himself up, kept going, stumbled repeatedly. He did not know where he was going and hardly cared. When he finally paused atop a hill to catch his breath, he saw a valley ahead . . . yes, a familiar valley and that dark patch on the ground must be Wang. He rushed down the slope, but as he approached the sleeping figure he slowed his pace. "Wait a minute," he said to himself, "could my jangled nerves have played a trick on me?" Against the commonplace reality of their camp and his own rumpled bedding, the headless woman was beginning to seem a figure out of a fading nightmare. Wang would tease him mercilessly if he knew how frightened he was. Wei, however, was too excited to lie down and keep still. He waited a while and then reluctantly shook Wang's shoulder. Bleary-eyed, Wang asked, "What's the matter? You look pale."

"Well," Wei said, "I can't sleep. My imagination is overwrought." He recounted what he thought had happened but tried to make light of it. By the end of the story, he was ready to apologize to his friend for waking him when his friend said, "Well, what's so strange about that?" and nonchalantly removed his head.

I could feel the chill in the night air as I finished my tale. David listened. He placed his sherry glass on a rock and then slowly raised both hands to his head. That gesture, I am happy to say, broke the spell. How solid and reassuring reality can be!

I finished the fieldwork for my dissertation in 1954. In 1962 David again joined forces with me, this time in New Mexico, where I had been teaching since 1959. My life status had changed little since I first met David in Arizona. I remained single. The only change of any note—progress, if you like—was from being a graduate student to being a junior member of the faculty. David, meanwhile, had married and was the proud father of two little girls. He brought his family with him. We renewed our friendship and continued to develop our common interest in the desert. But I couldn't help noticing some differences. An asymmetry had emerged. The first time we met, we met as two self-contained individuals. The second time, this was no longer quite the case. When he spoke with me, he still spoke with— well, me. But when I spoke with him, I addressed an enlarged personality, more diffuse and hence more difficult to target than the David I knew, for to the original man had been added other selves—his better self (as an older generation quaintly put it) and his offspring—his future selves. Even when I talked with him alone, unless it was about some technical matter, I was aware of these other presences that must be considered or consulted before he could commit himself or his time beyond strictly set limits. We had lost a certain spontaneity.

We still went on field trips. All the Harrises came along if the site was especially scenic or had an unusual past. One famous historical site was Chaco Canyon in northwestern New Mexico. Large, multistoried architec-tural ruins dating to the thirteenth century cover the floor of the canyon. We set out from Albuquerque in two cars: I in my little truck, David in his new English sedan. I led the way. We drove up the Rio Grande Valley and then followed the Rio Chama across the San Juan Mountains to a plateau, beyond which was our destination for the day—a little town called Cuba. My plan was that we would check into a motel there and start for Chaco Canyon the next morning. By the time we were on the dirt road that led out of the Rio Chama Valley, it was already dusk. David must have decided that he knew the way and that there was no point in following me. More-over, the children probably needed attention. I guessed these reasons. What happened was a beep from behind, then a rush of air as David's car overtook mine in a cloud of dust. I didn't want to be left too far behind, so I pressed down the pedal. But my truck was not made for speed (see fig. 9). The distance between us steadily widened. After a while, all I could see was the cloud of dust. Then, not even that. I was entirely alone in the deeply shadowed landscape.

In 1962 I was thirty-one—still young by the standard of academic life.

Fig. 9. Fieldwork and family fun in northwestern New Mexico, near Shiprock, February 1963. The picture was taken the day after the Harrises and I stayed in Cuba. Sarah, the Harrises' older daughter, sat next to the giant boulder. To the right is my little truck, which couldn't keep pace with the Harris family sedan.

More to the point, I still had unbounded enthusiasm for coming to grips with the world. Pleasure in thinking, coupled with the belief that I was making progress, drove out most competing social or biological goals and temptations. I lived and worked alone yet seldom knew loneliness. It didn't occur to me that, from society's viewpoint, my life could seem rather pathetic—without family and without intimate friends. What happened on the Chama road was this. As I strove to catch up with the Harrises, I felt alone for the first time—bitterly alone. Worse, I felt ridiculous. What on earth was I doing on that dirt road in New Mexico, chasing after a young family in its family car? I thought of turning the truck around and driving right back to Albuquerque. But of course, I didn't. Sanity returned. At the motel in Cuba, I found that the Harrises had already changed the baby, who was cooing in her cot. We were all ready for something to eat.

Shy people, unsociable people, or people like me whose need for sociability was repressed by an acute sense of their own oddness, may be expected to appreciate nature. Misfits find consolation among plants and animals that do not judge. But even there they are not entirely secure, for living things form communities; many are social beings that in their own worlds discriminate, include, and exclude. Only in the midst of mineral nature—desert or ice—can a human being feel entirely free from not only the actuality but even the awareness of social opprobrium.³

Do I like nature? In our postmodern, morally fluid society, the one rock that remains—the one moral imperative that is least likely to be challenged—is "Thou shalt love nature." I confess that I don't love or even much like nature if one means by that word biological life and little else, as so many young people in the environmental movement do. I am ambivalent about organic striving, the clever maneuvers of the selfish gene. That so much of the universe is "mineral" consoles rather than dismays me. I am by no means alone in this attitude. Our number, however, is small, as it must be if the species is to propagate and biological evolution to continue.

My mineral bias must be profound, for it is inscribed in my earliest memory. I was about three, and we lived in Tianjin, a city that can be quite cold in winter, cold enough for ice to form in the ponds. I took a nap every afternoon. Waking up made me bad tempered for, like most young children, I resented eviction from the Eden of sleep. Mother, you may recall, drew a motorcar in anticipation of my younger brother's tantrum. To appease me, my nurse did something even more imaginative. She filled an ashtray with water and put it on a ledge outside the window, exposing it to freezing temperatures. When she saw that I was about to wake up, she retrieved the ashtray, turned it over on a table by my cot, tapped it with the handle of a knife, and—lo and behold!—a sparkling ice sculpture fell out. To my young eyes, it was pure magic.

Mineral purity—anything that sparkles in the sun—remains for me a source of extraordinary aesthetic appeal. Now that I think of it, in my whole life I have bought only one totally nonfunctional object—a Tiffany glass apple. It now sits on a table in my living room. When the late afternoon sun shines on it, the crystal glass turns into a globe of light, patches of it brilliantly rainbow colored. I contemplate this mineral object from time to time, hypnotized by its beauty and happy to be reminded that not everything in God's creation is passion and struggle or suffers putrescent decay.

The enormous appeal of the desert took me by surprise. The desert, after all, did not figure in my childhood. It could not evoke ancestral memories. It was never my, or my family's, ecological niche. As a schoolboy in Australia, I knew that we lived on the edge of a great desert. But I never saw it. The first time I became aware of the splendor of arid land was when I took a train to California for graduate school. But the shock—the first real revelation—came a year later. During the winter break of 1952, some Chinese students and I decided that we should try that all-American avocation called camping. We set out for Desert Valley National Monument early one morning in the expectation that we would get there before total darkness set in. None of us had camped before, but we felt confident, for we were well equipped with tents, sleeping bags, and other paraphernalia thought necessary to the wilderness experience. Our car broke down somewhere south of Fresno. Fixing it took hours. By the time we reached Death Valley, it was late and dark. A strong wind rose that made our inexperienced attempts at tent raising futile. We gave up. I remember feeling discouraged. American students, I thought, would know how to raise a tent even in a blizzard; in any case, they would not have given up so easily. In the end, we simply slept in our sleeping bags, exposed to the wind, the dust, and, during calm interludes, the stars.

I awoke to lunar beauty. Fate, I like to think, had arranged its display to maximum effect. In the blinding dust and darkness of night, I had somehow managed to align my sleeping bag with the incline of an alluvial fan so that when I slipped into it my head was higher than my feet. Awake, all I needed to do was to raise myself a little higher, rest on my elbows, and a sweeping expanse of the valley's west wall was mine to behold—a phantasmagoria of shimmering mauves, purples, and bright golds, theatrically illuminated by the first rays of the morning sun. Extraterrestrial too were the saline flats on the valley floor and the ubiquitous stark sculptural reliefs. But even more unearthly was the calm, the hush. I looked in wonder. Anyone would. But it is a puzzle to me why I should feel not only wonder but an intoxicating happiness.

The next and last time I truly appreciated nature (as distinct from the nods of approval I regularly dispense from habit or good manners) occurred in Panama. I was there in the summer of 1959 to study its coasts.[4] Accessibility presented a challenge. The jeep I borrowed from the U.S. Navy took me to most places but not all that I needed to see. One hard-to-reach location was a sand spit that curved around a shallow bay. I was told that I could get there in only two ways. One was on the back of a donkey (a four-hour ride) and the other was by fishing boat. I opted for fishing boat. From a villager, I learned that if I went to a certain cove around noon, I would find people waiting to be picked up by a trawler. I could ride with them. I went to the cove at the designated time and found no one. I waited an hour. Still no one. I waited another hour. A couple of people came. Four hours or so later, a small crowd was gathered at the pier. We continued to wait. I detected no sign of impatience. People chatted merrily. The sun had set. But there was still no boat. When it finally came, the moon had already risen high in the sky. We piled into the boat. It moved out without further delay. The air was still, the water in the bay glassy smooth, except for the two rolls of waves parted by the boat's prow. Perhaps the passengers were tired, for they fell silent. I sat quietly with them, half mesmerized by the moonlight dancing on the water and half by the gentle putt-putt of the engine. A boy climbed up the tall mast and sat on the crossbar, his slender legs dangling in the air. He was framed by the cross, stark and black against the clear sky. Well, what can I say but that I was stricken by beauty?

I mean to evoke an image of nature. But there was that boy silhouetted against the night sky, and his presence made an important difference. Without him, I would still see the beauty, I would still want to retain an image of that mirror-smooth water, the moon, the dark line on the horizon that was the spit. But with that young human figure seated on the mast, the scene became for me more than just visually attractive but poignant and touching. The mood of that scene also was affected by what came after. In this respect, it differed from my other nature experiences, including the dramatic one at Death Valley. The magical view of Death Valley in early morning sunlight was circumscribed. What happened after—we got up to make breakfast, walked around the alluvial fan, quarreled over our next destination, and so on—did not cast a new light or shadow on that experience. This was not the case in Panama.

A festival was in progress on the sand spit when I arrived. People were eating, drinking, and dancing. I stood by and watched. After a while, dizzy with fatigue, I left the crowd, the noise, and the glare of naked lightbulbs to seek out the night's soothing darkness. Among the dunes and scrub I found a patch of clean sand. I lay down on it and quickly fell into deep sleep. I awoke to someone shaking me by the shoulder. Because she looked stern, my first thought was to protest—to tell her that I wasn't in anyone's way. She was speaking to me in rapid Spanish, which I couldn't understand. It took me a while to gather that she wanted me to accompany her to her house. Curious, I did as I was bidden. In the house, I understood what she had in mind, for she pointed to a large bed. I was moved by her thoughtfulness. I lay down on the bed, and even though men, women, and children were laughing and chatting, moving in and out of the house, I quickly and gratefully sank back into oblivion. Hours must have passed. Again someone shook me by the shoulder. It was the same woman. This time, she did not merely look stern—she was stern and made gestures that could mean only one thing: "Get out!" Not knowing the local custom, it would appear that I had abused her hospitality by sleeping longer than I should, thus depriving her children of their turn.

I couldn't quite decouple the calm image on the boat from the noisy merry making and my little contretemps with the woman on the sand spit. They were adjoining sequences of the same adventure, strikingly different yet resonating with each other in expectation and in memory. And were they so different? Even in the silence of the boat, my experience of natural beauty was not altogether serene. The presence of the boy disturbed it. Over time, I was forced to conclude that, for me, beauty has to be inhuman—even inanimate—to be a balm to the soul. Thus my love of the desert.

Does this mean that I am incapable of appreciating human works—constructed environments? No, not at all. The city can have immense appeal for me. Strange as it may sound, I am drawn to it for the same reason that I am drawn to the desert. The appeal in both is a certain starkness—and, more than starkness, a crystalline splendor, a glittering inorganic majesty. I readily see myself standing with Wordsworth on Westminster Bridge, contemplating London and saying with him,

> Earth has not anything to show more fair:
> Dull would he be of soul who could pass by
> A sight so touching in its majesty:
> This City now doth like a garment wear
> The beauty of the morning; silent, bare,
> Ships, towers, domes, theatres, and temples lie
> Open unto the fields, and to the sky;
> All bright and glittering in the smokeless air.
> Never did sun more beautifully steep
> In his first splendour valley, rock, or hill;
> Ne'er saw I, never felt, a calm so deep![5]

The poet is watching a still-sleeping London, the majesty of which lies in its ships and buildings, all "bright and glittering" under the morning sun. That was and probably still is the best time to see London as a work of art. Dusk would be less suitable, for in that hour traffic noise and the swarms of Londoners on their way home could be distracting. As for night, the city disappeared from view altogether in Wordsworth's time, except for a few poorly illuminated streets, or unless the moon was full. We too easily forget how recent was the dominion of darkness, first overcome by gas, then by electricity. The adage "city life is night life" would have been incomprehensible before 1800. Now even provincial towns can glitter after dark. What they present to view are not so much architectural mass and volume as patterns made up of colored dots, diagonals, and rectangles, set against a backcloth of velveteen black. We have grown accustomed to this Mondrian beauty and care no more for it than farmers ignorant of the enthusiasms of the Romantic movement cared for the picturesque qualities of their hills and dales.

In Madison, Wisconsin, I taught a course in which we examined the relationship between physical setting (natural or built) and quality of life. Before we began, I would ask students to jot down the environment that has the greatest appeal for them, one that has contributed most to their quality of life. Over the years that I gave this course in Madison—and earlier, in Minneapolis—students overwhelmingly designated a wilderness area or the countryside as their favorite place and almost never the city. Yet most of them were city people. They grew up in Minneapolis, St. Paul, or Madison, all noted for their fair appearance and livability. Moreover, college-age students aren't just passive habitants; they are the city's boldest explorers; they are the ones who discover tucked-away coffee shops, the friendliest taverns, the specialized bookstores; they are the ones who stay up all night, see the city in a blue haze of inebriation and hot jazz, and, hours later, after the third cup of coffee, empty streets bathed in celestial early-morning light. Yet they dismissed the city as though it has nothing to do with their satisfactions and happiness. Young Americans surprise me by their irrationality. For all their exuberance and extroversion, for all their belief in engaging reality frontally, they nevertheless allow what they read in class—literary effusions of dead nature-writers that find support in their own experience only by the occasional trip to a mosquito-infested forest—to overrule their day-to-day encounters with the exciting and the genial in urban space.

"Look out of the window from an upper floor in Science Hall," I would say to them in exasperation. "Doesn't the view remind you of good times?" I would plead with them to consider even the obvious, how on an average afternoon they might study with a friend in Memorial Library, later (but not much later!) walk the few steps across the fountain plaza to the student union, order beer at the Rathskeller, sit on the terrace that overlooks Lake Mendota, and stay long enough to see the sailboats float into the sunset. Winter offers a different set of contentments and raptures. The terrace is abandoned, trees become gaunt traceries on a gray sky, fountains are covered. But it is then that Madison, or any proud northern city, comes into its own. "Think of Madison in evening attire on a clear December night," I would hector. "From the top of Bascom Hill, after a late class in Birch Hall, you see something that is familiar yet remains a feast to the eye. In the foreground is the darkened campus mall. Beyond stretches State Street, its sidewalk trees decked with myriads of sparkling bulbs, its shop windows and signs sending hues of soft light on the banked snow, its buildings of different size and form—blacks and tinted grays—telescoped from where you stand into a pictorial composition, and at the other end of the street the brightly lit dome of the state capitol, towering over the horizon like a bloated moon."

The images that stay with me—ice, desert, sea, and city—are all a little lacking in human warmth. Their appeal is more to the spirit and imagination than to the needs and cravings of the body. These landscapes are either thinly peopled or unpeopled, and even the city is admired when it is nearly empty. To none does the word *intimate* apply. Aren't there homey places that I can recall? Yes, there are. But in contrast to sublime nature and the great city, I must make a conscious effort to recall them. This is not in itself surprising, for people generally do not take note of the sensorially complex and familiar—the all-enveloping cocoons of daily life. There is another reason for the meagerness of intimate images in my adulthood—living alone. Intimacy need not, of course, be with another person; it can be with an animal and even with an inanimate object, such as a warm sweater or a cozy room. Nevertheless, the emotional tone and aliveness in all things borrow heavily from the human: the dog can be a real companion only because we see it as more than an animal; the warm sweater "hugs," the house is alive with sights and sounds of welcome.

True human intimacy, sad to say, escapes me. Why not try surrogates? Why not keep a dog or a cat? Well, if I had a human family, I might well do so. But without the real thing, its huge challenges and rewards, I don't want to settle for second best. Pride or perversity is at work here. But there is something else: I don't want to hurt a dog's feelings by saying to it, "Well, I don't have a warm human body to pet, so you will have to do!" Absurd, isn't it?

As a child I was naturally a member of a family, surrounded by grown-ups who catered to my needs, in the course of which I experienced various kinds of intimacy, not all of them (by the way) welcome. But my memory of what actually happened is unexpectedly deficient in detail. Why didn't cozy images of childhood rise up in my mind as they obviously did for, say, A. A. Milne? Could it be that, like all fortunate children, I took support and attention for granted? True, my memory is not a total blank. I do remember recovering from pneumonia when I was about six years old. Pneumonia could have been fatal. I needed time to recuperate. Everyone knew that and so no guilt was laid on me. I wallowed in bed among my toys, day after day, while my brothers went to school. As I regained my appetite and felt stronger, I tried out a song that I had made up, with the ridiculous, reiterated words, "Dear old mom, dear old dad!"

Caring. This warm-puppy word has become sentimental and tacky with overuse. Yet I cannot do without it. Caring is a special kind of intimacy, most often and most tenderly experienced when we are little and have to be looked after and at all ages when we are sick. What was it like to be a child with aching limbs and high fever? Let me draw on the experience of John Updike, for mine, as I have noted earlier, was ambivalent. Updike puts it this way. A man sees a woman mounting the stairs to her sick child with breakfast on a tray and remembers

> those lost mornings when he, too, stayed home from school: the fresh orange juice seedy from its squeezing, the toast warm from its toasting and cut into strips, the Rice Krispies, the blue cream pitcher . . . the fever-swollen mountains and valleys of the blankets where books and crayons and snub-nosed scissors kept losing themselves, the day outside the windows making its irresistible arc from morning to evening, the people of the town travelling to their duties and back, running to the trolley and walking wearily back, his father out suffering among them, yet with no duty laid on the child but to live, to stay safe and get well to do that large something called nothing.

And then comes a line that makes the house itself a caregiver: "settling, ticking, clucking in its stillness, an intricately worked setting for the jewel of his healing."[6]

Sickness returns adults to dependency. Once more we need care by others, and we need a nurturing place in which to regain strength. A special quality of attentiveness (exemplarily chicken soup and plumped-up pillows) is given the sick. A special kind of intimacy is established with the sick room in the slow process of recovery. A special quality of thankfulness reaches out and covers the nurturing other, both persons and place. Humans may be uniquely privileged in these attitudes and feelings. For example, while all mammals look after their young, humans do so over an extended period. But perhaps an even more significant difference is that humans are capable of setting aside other duties to stay with their needy—the frail, the injured, and the unwell of whatever age. As the locus of recovery, the home is charged with a degree of affectional warmth that other primates—baboons, monkeys, and apes—cannot know.

I am fond of quoting the following remarks made by two distinguished anthropologists, S. L. Washburn and Irven DeVore. They produce an unforgettable picture in my album. "[When] the troop moves out on the daily round, *all* members must move with it or be deserted. The only protection for a baboon is to stay with the troop, no matter how injured or sick he may be. . . . For a wild primate a fatal sickness is one that separates it from the troop, but for man it is one from which he cannot recover even while protected and fed at the home base."[7]

A man who has always lived alone cannot know home in all its wealth of meaning. I do not know what it is like to have a leisurely breakfast with a loved one on a bright Sunday morning. I do not see children's fingerprints on the drawing-room curtain or their outgrown bicycles in the basement. Home, for me, is architecture. Yet how intensely human architecture— mere rooms and furniture—can be! This is hard for the rational mind to understand. Even more of a mystery is that a new place of residence can seem human right away, when one would have thought that the passage of time is essential. In 1952 I fell in love with the desert at first sight. In 1983, less dramatically, I felt instant affection for my apartment. That was the year I came to Madison to teach. The real estate agent showed me a dozen places, but none struck me as suitable. As the day wore on, I grew desperate enough to invent excuses to say to myself, "Yes, this will do, this must surely do." The last stop was at an abandoned elementary school, next to Lake Monona, that was being converted into condominiums. Workmen were still putting in the windowsills and retouching the woodwork. The floor was covered with spilled paint, dust, and protective canvas. Despite these forceful signs of an unfinished state, the rooms had for me a certain lived-in quality. Helping to create the illusion were the bricks exposed on the kitchen wall. They suggested age, a touch of autumnal mellowness, as did the late afternoon sunlight pouring in through the windows. No doubt my memory was also stirred—the time dimension stretched—by odor, for among the first things I noticed upon entering the apartment was the faint fragrance of tobacco. A workman was taking a break. He leaned out the window with the stub of a cigarette cupped in one hand.

To a child of the professional middle class living in the 1930s and 1940s, home was not only nurture and intimacy but also glamor, because certain parts of it—or certain social functions in it—were closed to him until he came of age. Glamor in the home meant late nights, cigarette smoke, people conversing and laughing. I remember stealing downstairs whenever I could to poke my nose into the brightly lit dining room where my parents and their guests, having just finished their meal, passed around Goldflake cigarettes. These came tightly packed in a cylindrical can. To remove a cigarette, one tugged at a paper hook with long handle that the manufacturer had provided. On those rare occasions when I was allowed to stay up late and make an appearance among adults, I would go to them one by one with the offer to extract a cigarette from the pack. They thanked me, leaned back in their chair, lit up, and chatted, a picture of contentment. Memory of this kind gives home a meaning beyond architecture and comfort. It would have lain deeply buried but for my unexpected encounter with cigarette fragrance in the Doty School building. I felt, fleetingly, that, even for a bachelor keen on guarding his privacy, the social possibilities of home remained a lure.

Although Doty School's apartments have been totally redone and are therefore new, its handsome shell has not been changed and is old. I have moved into a place that does, after all, have a past. The way the building's past consoles me, making my unit in it more homelike and human,

Fig. 10. Here I am, admiring Laura Komai's quilt, which hangs on my bedroom wall at Doty School Condominium, Madison, Wisconsin. The sun pours through the skylight to illuminate a large bench at which I read or write in my commonplace book. To my left is my sister-in-law Manlin.

prompts me to reach a broad conclusion, namely, that the memory that lends aura to place need not be from one's own past and unique to oneself. It can draw on magical moments known to other people in other times and places. Sleepless at night, I find peace—almost as good as sleep—by looking at the moonbeam coming in through the skylight; when it rains, I listen to the raindrops tapping on the window panes and slip, before I know it, into luxurious oblivion. Light from the night sky evokes the enchanted world of a child. Rain beating on the window evokes security, the kind that everyone's first home (mother) used to provide. These are the universals. One recognizes them almost anywhere. They are independent of the physical details of place and its local history. Dependent on such details and local history is the following experience. If I still can't sleep, I resort to an imaginative exercise that depends on my apartment's being in a building that was formerly an elementary school. I pleasantly hallucinate the voices of children attending class, for who knows? Where my head now lies may be where a child once sat.

The affection that I so quickly felt for my apartment has deepened with the passing of the years (see fig. 10). I now see it as almost alive. Each time I leave for an overnight trip, I pause at the door to check whether I have left anything behind—the sort of prudent step that I may take anywhere, at the door of a hotel room, for instance. But I also pause to say good-bye. My eyes settle fleetingly on the kitchen table with its imitation Tiffany lamp, the settee with its plumped-up cushions, the rows of alphabetized CDs, the books that I have accumulated over the years, the pile of magazines still waiting to be read. How calm and sweetly reassuring they are! They seem to say, "We will always be here for you." And that's one thing that can be said about the house and its material objects. They remain in place, they are stable. They are an anchorage in the midst of life's unceasing change. They are, in a sense, me and will briefly embody the real and best part of me after my death.

4

Intimate: From Justice
to Love

THE PICTURES that I offer now are troublesome to me, for they touch more directly on my character, including its deficiencies. Why make the effort? Is it that I can't resist the itch to show the scar on my stomach in the manner of Lyndon Baines Johnson, who led the country into new directions of exhibitionism? I am in a bind, for if this self-sketch is to be honest—psychologically true even if not all the details are accurate—I cannot avoid a confessional note. On the other hand, as a creature of my generation, undressing in public would be out of character. I intend to resolve the bind by indirection: that is, I shall draw on other people's honesty and eloquence to cover my lack of both. There! Already I have raised the hem of my shirt to expose a scar.

Cowardice and verbal inadequacy are not, however, the sole reasons for my reticence. I feel a reassuring oneness with other people when I find that even my most intimate, anguished, socially inadmissible emotions and desires are known to others. I am not alone. Stricken by a feeling that leaves me desolate, I say to myself, "Well, I bet I can find even that somewhere in Memorial Library." That confidence comes from experience. Kindred souls—indeed, my selves otherwise costumed—turn up in books in the most unexpected places. Discovering them is one of the great rewards of a liberal education. If I quote liberally, it is not to show off book learning, which at my stage of life can only invite ridicule, but rather to bathe in this kinship of strangers.

Justice. Children acquire a sense of fairness early. I was about five years old when I was given a little notebook and a pencil. I couldn't write, but I pretended to. One day, an uncle saw me scribbling. He asked to have a look. I showed it to him. "What are these little crosses about?" I replied indignantly, "They mark the occasions when my brother hit me." My uncle was not amused. He said I shouldn't harbor ill feelings. I should be able to forgive and, if not that, then come forward and confront my brother openly. Looking back, I can now see that my uncle had given me quite a hard lesson in morality and justice. I took it to heart. But I retained a strong sense of what was my due.

I made a point of behaving well, even selflessly, but if, despite my good intentions, I was reprimanded for what seemed to me a minor infraction, I became irrationally resentful. When I was about fifteen, we lived in London. Mother was in bed, recovering from flu. We—my father, brothers, sister, and I—sat around her. I had the happy thought of bringing toast and tea up to her from the kitchen, which was located two flights down in the basement. I made the tea and poured it into a cup, buttered the toast, cutting it into thin slices. I carried them up, precariously, without a tray. To free a hand so that I could open the door, I shoved the cutlery under my arm. Father saw what I did and quickly criticized me, presumably because he considered my action unhygienic. Poor Father! He had no idea that a reprimand so lightly offered would inflict a permanent wound. Even at the time I knew that it was just a slap on the wrist and perhaps deserved. Nevertheless, it confirmed my sour teenage view of life, namely, that even without front-page disasters, daily life could be out of joint, soiled, and unjust.

Children have a keen sense of their own dignity. They are also highly egocentric. The two propensities feed into each other. How can they treat me this way! Why am I getting a smaller piece of the pie? Moral education consists of persuading children to move away from self to others, to social obligations, and, finally, to an impersonal conception of justice. Father did his best to impart to us values of fairness that he considered traditional to Chinese society but that, for him, were reaffirmed by notions of equality and democracy that he had picked up in the United States. Unlike the caste system of India, Chinese social stratification was not rigid. Scholars were at the top of the four traditional classes; the others were made up of farmers, artisans, and merchants, in that order. Scholars were self-evidently not a hereditary group: they achieved their high status through hard work. Anybody could be a scholar. That, at least, was what we children were given to understand. The stories fed to us were not (heaven forbid!) from rags to riches: merchants, after all, stood at the bottom of the hierarchy. Nor were the stories from woodcutter to president, for the Chinese had no great regard for political or military power. Rather, they were from water buffalo boy to scholar.

Theory and ideal notwithstanding, Chinese society of my time was rife with class distinction and class consciousness. Female children could still be bought, though illegally, and used as servants—in effect, slaves. The rich lorded it over the poor, as elsewhere in the world. Both by example and by teaching, Father and his cohort of well-educated young men combated inequality and injustice. We children learned the lesson: it would not have occurred to us to condescend to the poor. Indeed, we romantically envied the boy of peasant background whose intelligence and ambition shined through his cover of rags. It was not unusual for people of my parents' age and time to adopt, either formally or informally, poor but talented children. On those occasions when I found my parents' appreciation of me wanting, I sought escape into fantasy. The fantasy was not of a princely waif mistakenly brought up in a commoner household but of an adopted child of humble origins, whose exceptional qualities of mind were not sufficiently recognized.

In the 1950s, middle-class America showed little outward awareness of the implacable realities of ethnic and racial discrimination. I *was* aware and concerned, not because as a Chinese I experienced egregious discrimination but because I had the discerning eye of someone still new to the country. At Indiana University in Bloomington, where I taught between 1956 and 1958, I could readily see that the youths who attended my classes and the youths who worked in the town's stone-cutting industry lived in separate worlds; their mutual antagonism was palpable and artfully explored in a movie called *Breaking Away* (1979).

Within the university, some fraternity houses were opulent; others were merely wealthy or just well-to-do. Hierarchy among them was as evident as among Oxford colleges of differing foundation, patronage, and wealth. I expected snobbery at Oxford: having read Evelyn Waugh I would have been disappointed not to find it there. But I did not expect to find it in a midwestern state university. Bloomington showed me, as it were, a pure example of class distinction, for the people involved were all white and mostly male.

I left Bloomington for Chicago in 1958. In Chicago I lived at International House and became aware of how gender and race could sharpen class distinction in America. At International House, men and women occupied separate wings. They could visit one another only during specified hours, once a week. Just before the time for visiting, the men would take a shower and rush around naked in the corridors, opening and slamming doors, pretending to be shocked at the possibility of being caught in the buff by their girlfriends. What hypocrisy, I thought. For the men did not in the least mind walking around semi-naked in the presence of maids.

Maids, especially if they were black, simply did not exist for the white male students. When I brought up this behavioral discrepancy, my American acquaintances showed, first, incomprehension, then embarrassment, then annoyance. They found my observation in poor taste.

I felt mildly indignant at the biases and injustices of society. It did not occur to me to do anything. By the time of the civil rights movement of the 1960s, I was sufficiently engaged with American society to feel that I ought to do something—that I ought to join protest movements. Again, I sat on my hands. Lethargy and cowardice were no doubt factors. But they couldn't be the only ones, for even when protests became almost fashionable and were conducted by oratory and the pen rather than by marching through hostile crowds, I refrained. I refrained even when geographers found a vocation writing papers and books on social injustice. These works focused, first, on the exploited working class, then on women and the ethnic minorities, then on gays and lesbians, following trends and fashions set by society at large. For all their technical competence, I saw in them an underlying naïveté, which is to presume that the world can be divided into good guys and bad guys, with those having little power—workers, women, ethnics, homosexuals—in the role of good guys and with those having inordinate power—the ruling class generally, capitalists, patriarchs, white men, heterosexuals—in the role of bad guys. I abhor injustice as much as the next geographer. Sensitive to a fault when it is inflicted on me, I can also take it very hard when I see it inflicted on another. In any confrontation between two groups, ideologies, or points of view, my sympathy shifts to the losing side with the naturalness of water flowing downslope. That's Simone Weil's metaphor, which I like. I also like her characterization of justice as that "fugitive from the camp of victors." I want to flee if only because I cringe at any display of triumphalism, unless, of course, it is just fun or natural exuberance, as when fans whoop it up when their team wins.

One reason that I have not been able to throw myself into fighting the battles of social injustice, as many geographers have since the 1970s, is pessimism. Pessimism is no better excuse for inaction than cowardice and lethargy. But I am not offering an excuse, merely a reason—an explanatory factor. My pessimism in regard to what social justice can accomplish rests on my keen awareness of biological injustice. Biological injustice— that is, the inequalities in our biological endowment—remains and will continue to make us, as individuals, unequal in other people's eyes and even in our own.

Why have I been drawn, since childhood, to this particular form of injustice? The answer lies in my exposure to Chinese custom, which allows parents to show favoritism openly. Everyone knows that they favor the male over the female child. This particular bias, unjust as it is, doesn't distress me unduly, for I see it as resting on a social convention that can be righted over time, as society becomes less dependent on mere masculine strength for security and success. Other favoritisms are less easily altered. One *naturally* favors vitality over feebleness, courage over timidity, cleverness over stupidity, beauty over ugliness. The first set of qualities enjoys an evolutionary advantage over the second. Adding to the imbalance is that the first set also stands for spiritual and moral values. Saints are known for their vitality. Courage is moral, not just physical (fool)hardiness. A good person may not be clever, but it is hard to think of one that does not possess moral discernment, moral intelligence, a largeness of spirit that is also a quality of the mind; on the other hand, an evil person is fundamentally limited, narrow, stupid.

Growing up, I saw daily that the good-looking or quick-witted child received more smiles and nods of approval than did the plain or dull one. To nature's already generous gifts were added those of society. How grossly unfair! Yet that is how things are ordained, as I was to learn later in one of Jesus' famous hard sayings: "To the person who has, more will be given so that he has an abundance; but to the person who has little, even the little he has will be taken away from him" (Matthew 13:12). Human beings can, and have, fought against biological injustice. Enlightened parents try to compensate by showering more attention on the less endowed child. Enlightened society itself spends generously on the physically and mentally burdened. Even in capitalist America, a land supposedly given over to uninhibited competition, resources are lavished on the slow learner, the lethargic, or the ultrakinetic in public schools, with only a pittance left over to nurture the gifted. Europe is rightly famous for its welfare programs, yet it is the United States that has poured money into remodeling its public buildings and sidewalks for the benefit of a small minority of wheelchair-bound citizens. It may even be that Americans are more disposed to righting biological wrong than social wrong, because many see the former as a cruel blow of fate that could have struck them, whereas a lingering suspicion remains that the poor are poor because they are lazy.

Still, even as a child I felt that no human compensation could make up for nature's meanness. Yes, one can make improvements—raise ugliness to plainness, a sluggish mind or clumsy limb to one of passable competence, but from such a low and defective base one can never hope to feel life's vitality to the full, achieve a level of excellence that is a delight to others as well as to oneself, soar with the ease of a bird in flight.

A middle-class family like ours, influenced by Western values, will never admit that good looks matter or even that being male is a decisive advantage. In any case, I had no cause to worry in these regards. I was a male child and not bad looking. Moreover, I enjoyed an even temperament, which gave me winning ways that made me feel attractive and well liked. The greatest deficiency I sensed in myself was mental agility. I sensed it not because I conspicuously lacked mental agility but because the aspiring middle-class family so openly set it up as the outstanding measure of worth.

I must have been about five when Father gave me some sums to do. I worked at them confidently and showed him the result. He looked at my work and said, "Well, that's not right, and you've got the second one wrong too. But you have got the third one right, and the fourth, and the fifth. Three out of five—not bad." I started to cry, for I thought that with such a mediocre score I could never become an engineer, which was what Father wanted his sons to be. For some reason, Father would not allow me to forget this incident. He was to tell it again and again to his friends and to me as I grew up. He thought it a charming story and never knew how humiliating "three out of five" was to me. I was branded with that score.

I realized then that I would never be good at math but thought that with application and the help of good teachers I could eventually become competent. Some twenty years later, in 1958, I tested that belief. I went to the University of Chicago on a postdoctoral fellowship in statistics (yes, in statistics, not in geography). I was surrounded by math wizards, some only in their early teens, still in high school but taking graduate courses at the university by special arrangement. In their midst, I felt the utter dullard. My poor training in math was bad enough—I should have known better than to accept a postdoc on such a weak foundation. More humbling by far, however, was my awareness that even in those probability classes that required little prior knowledge, only native intelligence, I was the dullard. Mathematical statistics was too difficult, so I migrated to lower-level courses that required only high-school algebra and trigonometry. There, an equation that takes up just one line if calculus were used was decomposed into a sprawling paragraph riddled with summation signs. I could follow every step of that sprawl without understanding in the least its real message, which led me to conclude that in any world where mathematics was a condition of responsible citizenship—and aren't we moving into such a world?—I would find myself permanently disenfranchised.[1] No well-meaning society could right this wrong.

I have taught at the university level for more than forty years. Each time I walk into a classroom, I assume that the students are about equally well prepared and about equally intelligent. By the middle of each semester I am shocked once more into the realization that this is not the case. If poor preparation is the cause of low achievement, I am not overly concerned, for the student can always be persuaded to work harder. Nor am I put out if the cause is a lack of interest in my subject, for the student may well find excitement and shine in other subjects. What I cannot accept, despite repeated confrontation with the obvious, is that students differ markedly in general native intelligence. In every large class, I can count on having a few who attend class diligently, try hard, do every assignment, yet come up with a C. "What can I do to raise it to an A?" they ask. I mumble, for it seems to me that the honest but cruel answer is, "You should have chosen brighter parents." Their work is not bad, just depressingly mediocre: almost every sentence construction, every thought, is banal. By contrast, bright students may hand in an assignment that also earns a grade of C. Clearly these bright students have not done their homework. They try to wing it—to fly on native wit—and fail. But the point is that the wit is nevertheless there in the occasional happy turn of phrase, in the daring (if not quite relevant) metaphor, throwaway achievements that are beyond the best efforts of the dull.

Vitality is a gift of nature. Some have more of it than others. Intelligence itself is a species of vitality. Great scientists and writers possess, of course, a superior mind, but "mind," in them, seems not just a subtle and delicate instrument housed in the skull but more like a primal force—a potency of nature—that suffuses the entire body. C. P. Snow remembered seeing Einstein stepping out of the sea at a New Jersey beach like a bronzed god. Writers such as Hugo, Balzac, Emerson, Whitman, and perhaps even Dickens saw themselves as more than human, with powers and ambitions to match. Keats died young and might have looked sickly at times. Yet there can be no doubt that he was a lively presence, his liveliness manifested in facial expression, gesture, and speech but above all in his works—letters and poems.

For some reason I cannot quite fathom, the importance of vitality to any kind of achievement really and finally struck home when I read Alfred Russel Wallace's two-volume autobiography. I was then at my first job in Indiana. I suppose I turned to him because, as a budding geographer, I had an interest in my intellectual forebears. But the one incident in that work that stayed with me in all the ensuing years has nothing to do with the distribution of plants and animals or with what came to be known as the Wallace Line. It is a human incident that sharply contrasts the fate of two brothers. Alfred Wallace spent four and a half years (1848–1852) in the Amazon basin, drawn to it by "the wonders of insect life." A younger brother, Herbert, joined him in 1849 to see whether he too had a vocation in natural history. There was a note of desperation in the move, for Herbert had tried various jobs in England and had liked none of them. After a year in the tropics, it became clear that the study of nature was not his calling either. "He took little interest in birds or insects," Alfred Wallace wrote, "and without enthusiasm in the pursuit, he would not have been likely to succeed."

Later, Alfred returned to this point, as though he couldn't quite grasp his brother's lack of direction and drive. "His misfortune was that he had no thorough school training, no faculty for or love of mechanical work, and was not possessed of sufficient energy to overcome these deficiencies of nature and nurture." Herbert left the expedition and stopped by Pará (Belém) to board the ship that would return him to England, but he died of yellow fever while waiting in the disease-ridden port. He was twenty-two.[2]

Herbert lacked vitality. Alfred had plenty. Even if Herbert had lived, his life in England could have seemed anemic by comparison with his brother's worldwide travels and intellectual accomplishments. Talent is longing, desire, passion. "In Dante, *talento* means lust," Gerald Brenan notes. "The charge in the meaning of the word suggests that it is the strong desire to write or paint that creates the ability to do so."[3] Brenan confirms my belief that real talent, even in the purely mental sphere, has to be more than just a knack for doing something well. To matter, it must also be vitality—a surging, rechargeable, and periodically recharged power that some people have far more than others. This, to me, is a fundamental injustice, for at stake are not only success and fame but the very quality of day-to-day living, what it means to be alive.

Vitality is also virtue. Or, rather, it makes one important form of virtue—a largeness of spirit or generosity—possible, even easy, and because it can seem easy, it can also seem natural. That naturalness makes the generous gesture even more appealing and admirable. Let me illustrate with two stories.

As a student, I often rode Greyhound buses. It was an inexpensive way to travel and, moreover, an easy way for me to see layers of American society that I don't normally see. In the larger cities, the bus station swarmed with all sorts of people, but two sorts, more than others, captured my attention: frail old women and tough young punks. When the bus was ready for boarding, the old women, clutching tight their battered suitcases, rushed to the door, shoving other passengers aside. The young punks took their time, were often the last to board, and they seemed to carry nothing other than a music box and a comb, which they periodically ran through their greasy hair. In the bus, the nervous women commanded the youths to lift their bags onto the overhead rack, and—to my surprise—they obeyed instantly, with (it would seem) just a flip of their forearm. I wondered about their occupations. Were they apprentice mechanics, farmers, service-industry workers, trade school students, marine recruits, or even, as a sideline, gang members? Whatever they did for a living, however they might have behaved in their own neighborhoods, in the Greyhound bus they acted the gentlemen. They could afford to do so. The Greyhound world was one in which they moved with confidence and ease. They helped strangers in need with an offhand gallantry that seemed to me a pure example of noblesse oblige.

The second story is of an event that occurred many years later. Heavy snow fell for days in late November 1982. When I looked out the window of my tenth-floor apartment in downtown Minneapolis, I could see that the entire city was blanketed in white. Foolishly, I tried to drive to work; predictably, my car got stuck half a mile from my apartment building. Few vehicles were on the streets, and most were as immobilized as mine. I thought of abandoning my car, but just at that moment I saw someone waving at me from across the street. He had just pushed a vehicle free. He came over to say that he would give mine a push. The wheels spun, skittered forward, then found a patch of snow, packed but not yet turned into ice, on which they could establish a grip. My car was ready to run on its own power.

I offered the man a ride. I said that since I couldn't possibly make it to the office, I was returning to my building—the River Towers Condominium. He said that he was heading that way too, that he worked there as a mechanic. In the slow crawl home, I asked him where he lived. In St. Paul, he said, and added that he had had to abandon his own car a couple of miles back and that, as he trudged his way through the snow toward Minneapolis, he had helped as many stranded motorists as he could. I was struck by what he had done. It carried biblical undertones, although I am sure he wasn't thinking of the Bible or any Golden Rule at the time. Like Christ, he couldn't "save himself," but he could save others. In the car, I had to concentrate on my driving and so barely glanced at my rescuer. In the garage, I was able to look at him. I found a young man bursting with vitality. He smiled when I thanked him, exposing a set of perfect teeth. I thought of him, in a fit of fantasy, as an archangel temporarily put on earth to help stranded mortals.

I remember these two incidents because they exemplify a form of virtue that I greatly admire, though I do so with a touch of guilt, for I am drawn to it more by its beauty than by its exhibition of moral will. I also envy the young men's vitality. It is a gift of nature that I have always felt I lacked. I was a sickly child. My health improved in adulthood, but even then I never had the sort of exuberance that could be tapped to help others or just sweeten the atmosphere in social exchange. All too often, through lethargy, I professed ignorance rather than take time to give directions to a stranger lost in town or looked forbidding when a smile would have encouraged an insecure student. This is not a picture of me that I like: it corrodes my self-esteem. Can I do anything about it? Apply willpower? Willpower determinedly applied can sometimes substitute for vitality, but the effect is a certain grimness that is unattractive. I consider my deficiency of vital force a biological injustice. I resent it, for I know that I can be a better person— certainly a more appealing one—if only the "green fuse of life" would flow less sluggishly through my veins.

I associate vitality with physical courage, another quality I lack. Sensing this lack is a recurrent source of humiliation, for it has always seemed to me that no other human trait is more despicable than cowardice. When we were children and lived in Chongqing, we played soccer whenever we could. We made a ball of sorts by tying together a bundle of cloth. One day, Father gave us a genuine leather soccer ball. We were ecstatic: we played with it, ate with it, slept with it. The disadvantage, from my point of view, was that it was hard. I didn't want it to smash into my chest or face. I was more than a little afraid of it. To hide my fear, I offered to be the goalkeeper, which would make me the target—the concerted target— of aggression. When a ball came zinging my way, or when a boy, carrying the ball, threw himself at me as though he were a projectile, I blocked ball or boy with my body in a rush of suicidal madness. This was not bravery. I could do it only by persuading myself that this was the end, that I would not survive the onslaught and so would never have to face it again.

Why be goalkeeper rather than play a position that gave me better control over the direction of the game? Once more the answer is my lack of vitality. As goalkeeper I more or less stayed put. I did not have to run with the ball, hurl myself forward, rush all over the field. There is such a thing as passive courage: it means holding one's ground. But it is active courage I admire—the courage of action, of movement and projection—male courage, if you like. I could never throw a ball properly. This is said to be a gender distinction: girls do not throw well because they use only the strength of their arm; boys, by contrast, use their whole body—they thrust their whole body forward, risking imbalance and a fall. I was unwilling to take that risk. In all games that involved a ball, I had to hide the shame of not being able to throw properly.

In the end, courage is more than just physical vigor, throwing oneself

71

daringly into space. It is also the ability to act decisively, with sangfroid, in a critical situation. There again I doubt I have courage. But I don't really know, for I have never been tested. Early on in my stay in Minneapolis, I read a report in the back pages of the newspaper that left an indelible mark on how I see life and its unpredictable challenges. The report was of a robbery on Hennepin Avenue. "I was with my wife and this guy came on us with a gun. He held it on her and that frightened me, but I didn't do anything, I couldn't. But somehow I kept calm. Then he put the gun on my head and before I knew it I was on my hands and knees crying and pleading. I cried about how my kids needed me and how I gave him everything we had and I just fell apart. I fell absolutely apart," the man told a reporter from the *Minneapolis Tribune* (September 23, 1970). The man was rescued and suffered no injury at the time other than a plunge in self-esteem.

I read Albert Camus's novel *The Fall* in 1957, when it first appeared in English translation. One cold evening, a man is crossing a bridge and hears a splash. Someone has fallen into the canal. The man who hears the splash can swim, but he does not attempt a rescue. Instead, he debates the pros and cons of taking action until it is too late to do anything. That sounds like me. What is not me, and can only be me in romantic fantasy, is the heroic action of Lenny Skutnick. On January 13, 1982, an Air Florida plane crashed into the icy Potomac River. Skutnick dived into it. At great risk, he saved a woman's life. The hero himself had to be taken to the hospital, for his body temperature had dropped dangerously low in the rescue attempt. When he eventually went home, he was bombarded by questions from neighbors and reporters. Why did he do it? How was he able to muster the courage to jump in? Skutnick seemed puzzled. He said: "She was going under. I was right there watching. She was going to drown if no one moved. I jumped in."[4]

In the shrug of the shoulder I find an attitude toward life that is most admirable. Skutnick and other heroes seem genuinely surprised by the fuss, as though sacrificing oneself for a stranger is perfectly natural. Thus far, I have stressed heroism on the spur of the moment: one moment one is driving in the comfort of one's car, looking forward to toasting before a fire at home; in another instant, one is splashing about in the icy Potomac, trying to keep a struggling woman afloat. And this violent shift of scene is brought about not by fate but one's own disposition and will. However, it goes without saying that sudden challenge is not the only test of courage, which can be manifested in many other ways, including the deliberative way of a planned enterprise. Consider the case of Guy Willoughby. One day in November 1989, "he shed the natty suit that he has frequently worn in Kabul [Afghanistan], dropped to his hands and knees off a highway north of here, and worked his way through a Soviet minefield. Using a metal detector, a probe and his hands, Mr. Willoughby, a former Guards officer in the British Army, lifted enough mines to clear a narrow path. That done, the twenty-nine-year-old Englishman and a companion, Paul Jefferson, cleared another, smaller minefield nearby. Back in Kabul, Mr. Willoughby, great-grandson of a former viceroy of India, departed for a vacation in England, where his passions include horse breeding and polo."

So reported the *New York Times* of December 3, 1989. I also read all the front-page news that day but no longer recall it. This back-page item will remain with me forever. Why did Guy Willoughby do it? Well, one reason is that the Afghans themselves would not volunteer. Another is noblesse oblige—a high-born Englishman's sense of obligation toward a country that the British have repeatedly fought over and patronized. Again, what I find especially praiseworthy in this act of courage is its lack of strain, its message that shedding one's natty suit to crawl on hands and knees over a minefield north of Kabul and then flying back to England for a game of polo is what life is about—what being alive in the full sense of the word means.

And moral courage? Am I also below par in that regard? Yes, if courage is a lionheartedness that reveals itself whether the challenge is physical or moral. After all, what is at risk is the same—life. This is obvious in acts of physical courage, but acts of moral courage also threaten life, for they court isolation from fellow humans, on whose support one's well-being and, ultimately, life depends. Malcolm Muggeridge is a hero to me if only because he repeatedly told the truth as he saw it, even if this meant the ostracism of his peers or losing his job, as happened more than once. Since I am an academic who constantly feels the pressure of activist students to support their cause or buttress their point of view, I am particularly impressed by Muggeridge's ability to withstand such pressure, which was at its height in the 1960s.

In 1966 Muggeridge was elected rector of Edinburgh University by the Student Representative Council, no doubt for his reputation as a maverick and an outspoken critic of the British establishment. The job of rector was almost entirely ceremonial; its one designated nonceremonial obligation was to pass students' wishes and concerns on to the university's governing body. Well, in 1967 the students wanted to have free pot and birth-control pills on campus. Muggeridge received their request but, instead of dealing with it through the usual channels, he gave his response in his Annual Rectorial Address on January 14, 1968. Normally, rectors used this great public occasion to play to the gallery, especially to the students' gallery, for they were, after all, elected by students. This time, the new rector spoke like an outraged Old Testament prophet. He said that he would have under-standing for almost any act of insubordination against the run-down, spiri-tually impoverished society that was Britain. But rather than direct righ-teous anger against it, "how infinitely sad; how, in a macabre sort of way, funny, that the form of [student] insubordination takes should be a de-mand for pot and pills, for the most tenth-rate sort of escapism and self-indulgence ever known! . . . The resort of any old, slobbering debauchee anywhere in the world at any time—dope and bed."[5]

Would I, decked in rectorial or professorial robe, dare to face the shock of disappointment and disapproval—the sullen silence, the hisses and boos—when, by offering the usual pablum of uplifting rhetoric, I can fill my ears with waves of applause? I suspect not. What may seem puzzling is that I am less bothered by moral cowardice than by physical cowardice. The key to the puzzle, I suspect, is this. From time to time, a friend is criticized by someone whose good opinion I not only value but need. Rather than acquiesce or just remain silent, I almost always manage to rise to the occasion and defend the absent friend. I have never, however, been tested physically: if a mugger attacks someone who happens to be in the same public space as I, would I rush to the victim's defense? I don't know, and I live with the uneasy feeling that I may not.

As to saying something unpopular in a public forum, I have been tested and found wanting. For example, in the 1980s, despite my doubts about my university's slogan, "Design for Diversity," which seemed to have dis-placed the older one of "Sifting and Winnowing for Truth," I did not take to the floor of the Faculty Senate to object. If I had, I would have encoun-tered a wall of incomprehension and anger. My lack of courage in this context is shameful, far more so than if I had failed to defend a man or woman against an armed mugger. For I have never claimed physical cour-age or competence. But as a university teacher, my job is to risk unpopular-ity and reputation for the glimmers of truth—including the truth about the nature of the university—that are given to me to understand. Tenure is established for no other purpose. What complicates the picture a little and so provides me with a tattered cover is my temperamental inclination to see the world from another's point of view, to grant that my opponent may have a case, however misguided.

This ability to see the other person's point of view, feel his or her needs and passions, is generally considered a virtue—a self-denying act of the imagi-nation. The ability may even have a biological base: women rather than men, the introverted rather than the extroverted, are better endowed with it. However, to a greater degree than the virtues of physical drive and courage, the virtue of sympathetic understanding can be deepened and expanded with practice. It is educable, potentially within reach of everyone who desires it. For that reason, I am not too troubled by whatever initial inequality may exist. Moreover, in this power to place oneself in another's shoes, I do not feel deficient. Indeed, I believe I score above average.

For evidence I can draw upon a painful childhood experience. When my older brother was eleven, he sat for a difficult entrance exam to Nankai Middle School. The math tests were especially tough. My brother dejectedly told our parents that he did not think he did well. I overheard the bad news and started to cry. Mother said in exasperation, "Why are *you* crying when it was your brother who took the exam?" I couldn't answer her. I suppose what happened was that I became my brother. I entered wholly into his anxiety and disappointment. No doubt my distress was prompted in part by my realization that in another year I too would have to sit for the exam. But I don't think that was entirely it. What crushed me were not dark clouds in the future but rather the present gloom—my brother's and therefore mine. I remember this incident clearly because, again, Father would not allow me to forget. I was never sure when he would bring it up. Whenever he did, I felt that he had exposed a risible weakness in me.

I must have been a lonely child, for I often played a game that lonely children play, which is to imagine what it is like to be someone else. I could play this game anywhere, but my imagination was never more stimulated than when I sat in the glassed-in porch of our Sydney home and watched the cars moving like toys on the other side of Rose Bay. I would pick a car arbitrarily and imagine how the world might look to a passenger in it. I not only put myself in the location of the passenger, I also imagined myself to *be* that passenger—an Australian boy driven to his cricket match, a grown man on his way to a business meeting, and so on. I wanted to see another person's point of view, feel how he feels. Empathy came naturally to me, but I also cultivated it, turning it into something more socially and morally productive—sympathy.

Commiserating with another's troubles is a worthy sentiment but one that is not all that difficult to call forth. More challenging is to rejoice in someone else's success and happiness, especially when that success receives public recognition of the sort that we ourselves would like to have. Now, there can be no doubt that, generally speaking, parents are happy when their children are happy and successful. But parents see their children as extensions of themselves. They are no more likely to envy the success of their children than writers the success of their books. Parents are not supposed to talk about their children too often, the idea being that other people are not really interested. Maybe not. If so, then I am an exception, for I like to listen to the success stories of my friends' children.

As I listen, I put myself, now in the children's shoes, now in the parents' shoes, and so acquire a happiness of my own in two flavors. This sounds like a claim to high-mindedness, but there really isn't much to it, for three reasons. One is that I have no children of my own. If I had and they did poorly, I would be hard put to rejoice in the gloating of other parents. Second is my bleak view of human nature—my pessimism. I see so little of people genuinely happy in another's success that I light up when I do see it, even if it depends on an element of possessiveness, as is the case of not only parent and child but also of teacher and student—"Oh, *my* student does so well, what about yours?" Third is the romantic turn of my imagination, which inclines me to regard children as God's handiwork—unique creations put into the world for everyone to enjoy, if only one knows how, rather than as the appendage and property of a particular parent or teacher.

I have learned to extend to human beings generally this way of seeing young people (children and students) as aesthetic objects and public art. Human beings are aesthetic objects of a special kind in that they can literally speak for themselves. I want to know about them as I would paintings, sculptures, and musical compositions. I stand silent before a painting, wondering how it has acquired its appeal, what it "says." In the company of people, I look and listen, wondering how they come to be what they are, how they see the world. I prefer to be silent, the one who is acquiring rather than dispensing knowledge. Of course, in the classroom I have to speak and speak at length. But in social gatherings, when I speak at all it is usually to ask a question or to point to an irony or paradox, the purpose of which is to elicit comment, to restart a conversation.

From this, the conclusion may be drawn—correctly—that I am a nice guy, knowledgeable yet attentive to other people's views, a good person to have at a party or in a discussion group. Unfortunately, the niceness and modesty have a less worthy side. It could be that I have no developed intellectual position or strongly held moral principles of my own. Or, if I do have them and refrain from pushing them because of good manners, it may be that the good manners themselves are suspect: that is, they derive not from strength but from insecurity—the social insecurity of the foreign guest, visitor, immigrant. Someone like Margaret Mead can afford to be assertive, blunt, even rude, for she is undeniably a daughter of the house. I, by contrast, am only a guest of forty years' standing who still feels it politic to defer to the opinions of native-born Americans. It somehow reassures me to know that Isaiah Berlin too was troubled by his tendency to bend over backward to see his adversary's point of view, his fatal desire to please—a weakness that he attributed to being a Jewish Russian expatriate in an Anglo-Saxon culture. All those awards and honors he accumulated in England, with hardly ever an adverse notice, were they all due to the force and originality of his work, or did charm—the soothing, civilized tone he brought into any controversial topic—also play a role?[6]

Taking pleasure in another's satisfaction or success may contain a masochistic element that is less than wholesome. I worry over my selflessness for that reason. How did the masochistic element enter my personality? I suspect that I was born with it. I have never been very assertive. Shy as a child, I remain somewhat reticent in adulthood and in a position of responsibility. In the company of younger people, especially, I am disposed to subdue my own will, reveal my uncertainties, even as I am expounding a viewpoint. This gentle trait makes me approachable and sympathetic— desirable qualities in a teacher. At my retirement banquet, a former student recalled that he and I ate at a Chinese restaurant in San Francisco several years ago and that during dinner I kept urging him to eat. I was surprised that he should remember and bring up such an inconsequential detail. Yet, on reflection, he was right to do so, for he was making a point about my personality. A reason, I now realize, that I frequently go out to have coffee or a meal with students is that I like to see them eat. I like to see them and their world grow, as they consume pasta in marsala sauce, carrot cake, good books, and good ideas. I want them to consume me.

However, selflessness carried too far can rub so harshly against one's natural egoism that it brings about its opposite—explosive, angry demands for recognition. I see the danger and try to quit at the first sign of strain. But why is exaggerated selflessness even a temptation? In my case, the answer is that society has actively promoted my natural bent. Society says selfishness is bad. As a child, I very much wanted to be good. The opportunity to be selfless and good came in the course of a typical Chinese meal—a communal affair at which everyone feeds off the same set of dishes placed at the center of the table. In our family of six, we regularly had four dishes to share. The problem was that, more often than not, only one dish was the favorite. Although we had a servant to cook our meals, from time to time Mother did a star turn in the kitchen, the outcome of which was one dish that all four children ravenously desired. There was never enough to go around.

What to do? The crudest step was to dive into the dish and eat as much as possible before others objected. I tried that but found it too humiliating. Another step, more subtle, drew on a psychological technique: one made a show of restraint in the expectation that it would encourage others to do likewise. At a critical moment, one would say offhandedly, "Oh, since none of you seem to want more of this stuff, I will help myself," and then, suiting action to the words, pour the remains onto his own plate. While I appreciated this step's skilled timing and flair, I did not take it up, for it still offended my self-image. In the end, what did I do? Well, I tasted the favorite dish, complimented Mother, and thereafter ate as little from it as possible without drawing attention to my abstinence. The result was a boost to my pride, a Luciferian defect in my character that was the obverse of my need for self-denial. But let me be fair to myself. I could also feel emotion of a wholesome kind as I watched my siblings enjoy Mother's cuisine, especially my younger brother, who loved food.

Selflessness makes for happiness. It pays. I try to draw on the lesson I learned in childhood, minus the masochistic excess. On the whole, it has worked well. Rather than fester in frustration over what I do not have—spouse, partner, children, love—I turn my attention to the happiness of people who do have them, live imaginatively in their plenty, and so appropriate it for my own. But unrelieved surrogate living exacts a heavy toll: it means a life in which even the best parts are contentment and satisfaction rather than unbuttoned joy; it means a world that constantly threatens to turn gray. Is it any wonder that I can idolize vitality, go overboard in my yearning for the irrepressible rush and glow of life?

Of all the biological injustices, the most public is physical appearance. As soon as we see someone, we make a judgment: he or she is good-looking, plain, or ugly. By contrast, an individual's other features—personality, intelligence, the moral virtues—are below the surface and can be appraised fairly only upon closer acquaintance. What makes the injustice even greater is that physical appearance is also powerfully emblematic; it suggests—it stands for—other qualities. Seeing a person for the first time, we may already conclude that she or he is bright or slack-witted, rash or prudent, trustworthy or of doubtful trustworthiness. We may be wrong—appearance can mislead—yet most of us unknowingly go by it, for it is too convenient a short-cut to knowledge to give up; moreover, most of the time our quick initial judgment turns out to be not far off the mark—or so we like to think.

The harsh saying noted earlier—"to the person who has, more will be given, but to the person who has little, even the little he has will be taken away"—probably applies to all endowments. Without doubt, it applies to beauty. Already a great good, it invites the attribution of other goods—moral elevation, for example; by contrast, ugliness, already a heavy burden, is burdened further with presumptions of evil. Is it any wonder that

Montaigne said, long before social scientists caught on, that "the first distinction that ever existed among men, and the first consideration that gave some preeminence over others, was in all likelihood that of beauty?"[7]

Viewing people as aesthetic objects can create a moral problem. That some individuals are clearly more pleasing to look at than others means that the favored may be unthinkingly accorded not only greater aesthetic appreciation but also greater respect as overall superior beings. An error of judgment—an intellectual error—can thus occur that affects the disposition of favors at all levels, down to the minute, though not unimportant, one of smiles and nods. I try to guard against the error. I try all the harder when I am with students—people over whom I have some influence. In making an effort to discount physical appearance, I stand on higher moral ground than those Chinese parents who openly and unjustly show favor to their good-looking child. But I don't always succeed. The fair of countenance irresistibly turn me on; they energize me by their mere presence. The ugly, by contrast, drain me of vitality, perhaps because of my constant effort to disregard what my eyes see.

But let me not exaggerate the challenge. All my life, I have lived in school or college communities, surrounded by the young and pleasing of form. Rarely do I see the plain, much less the ugly. When I envision a human being, I automatically envision a limber young man or woman. He or she *is* humanity for me. That people come in all sizes and shapes—that the human species is highly polymorphic—is a fact that I tend to forget or repress. A visit to the core of a bustling metropolis is a shock, for there I am confronted by the whole range of human types. I feel I have entered a circus or carnival filled with exotica and grotesqueries—dwarfs and giants, the nimble and the ponderous (monkeys and elephants), and all oddments of shape, size, and kinetic agility in between—all worth watching but not to speak or sleep with.

At Borders bookstore, I sat in a corner chair to browse through a book on art. At that moment, a large woman came over and eased herself into a chair next to mine. I was captive to her presence, in particular to the way her white-dough flesh exuded in bulbous tumult from her tight shorts. I couldn't concentrate on my book. I had to leave and was ashamed to do so. But *she* felt no shame, no responsibility toward the aesthetics of the environment of which she was a part. Do we know that our physical appearance can powerfully affect our neighbor's well-being? No, or apparently not, according to Milan Kundera. In a novel, he depicts a woman whose "outfit seemed to make her behind even heavier and closer to the ground. Her bare, pale calves resembled a pair of rustic pitchers decorated by varicose veins entwined like a ball of tiny blue snakes." Another character,

Agnes, observes this and says to herself, "That woman could have found a dozen outfits that would have covered her bluish veins and made her behind less monstrous. Why hadn't she done so? Not only have people stopped trying to be attractive when they are out among other people, but they are no longer even trying not to look ugly!"[8]

Cultures differ in the importance they assign to human beauty. Publicly (though not privately, as I have noted) the Chinese assign little value to it: under the influence of Confucian moralism, good behavior matters, not good looks. Modern American culture would seem to worship the Body Beautiful, yet the Body Gross, increasingly common among a generally overweight population, exhibits itself with little sense of shame. Indeed, the grossness is flaunted as a sort of "in your face" dare. By contrast, the ancient Greeks treated human beauty with high seriousness, perhaps because they identified it with other human excellences. Beauty, to them, is a divine force, a blaze of sun against which mortals have to shade their eyes. The Greeks, even the old and wise among them, paid homage to the handsome youth. Another example of a culture highly sensitive to the aesthetics of human form is the African, more specifically, the cattle-herding culture in East Africa. "It is a good thing in Maasailand to show beauty when you possess it," says Tepilit Ole Saitoti. "Traveling in our land you would often see young warriors barely covered, walking with immense pride." But when they come of age, they cover themselves out of respect for the young. In public places, the eyes should be protected against unnecessary offense. When Tepilit Ole Saitoti came to the United States and visited Long Beach, California, he was shocked to see "flabby and wrinkled old men and women" walking around in bathing suits in total disregard for other people's sensibilities.[9]

Ugly buildings and streets have about them the smell of death. We feel called upon to erase, rebuild, or beautify. But what if we human beings are the ugly ones in the environment? How can we change ourselves? Ought we to? Ought we spend time and resources on what is so often deemed, in a high moral mood, to be just a surface aspect of our being? I am not happy with my own sensitivity to people's physical appearance, for while it often gives me pleasure, it can also make me miserable, all the more so when I recognize the fundamental unjustness of my response. And the response can be overwhelming. I have already mentioned the woman at Borders. I reacted horribly even though she was not my environment, just an element in it. Suppose I am surrounded by people of exceptional ugliness? In Minneapolis, I waited for the elevator to take me to my tenth-floor apartment. It arrived. I got in. Soon several others entered and then even more pushed their way in until we were packed tight. The door closed. The elevator rose slowly. I couldn't move my arms, but I could turn my head. What was it that so quickly altered my state of mind for the worse? The bluish pallor of the fluorescent light? The staleness of the air? The drooping flab of the human figures? The pasty blankness of faces seamed with age lines? The staring but unseeing eyes? The thin, pressed lips? In any case, I was horrified to be locked in with so much concentrated ugliness. I struggled to breathe, to be disengaged from my fellow passengers, to contain the rising tide of panic in me.

If this is how I occasionally see others, how do I see myself? As a child, the periodic pat on the head and the occasional compliment encouraged me to think that I was among the favored. In young manhood and even in early middle age, I continued to regard my appearance as a notch or two above plainness. Nevertheless, I wondered from time to time what my fate would be like, how I could affect other people, and how I might see the world, if I were not just plain but deformed or conspicuously ugly. For this reason, I was keen to read about John Merrick, nicknamed the Elephant Man, who suffered a genetic disorder that made him, in his surgeon Frederick Treves's words, "the most disgusting specimen of humanity that I have ever seen."[10] Merrick, who died in 1890, was an extreme case, however, so much so that he eventually became a celebrity and found friends among all manner of people, including royalty. His public appearances were, so to speak, grand entrances. People were prepared for him—prepared to see the patient and good man in the monster. So Merrick's life did not really answer my questions. I still wanted to know what it was like to walk into a room and see the barely suppressed shudder of distaste or, more mildly, a change of mood from ease to forced cheer.

In Albuquerque I found the hint of an answer in an experience that in itself was utterly commonplace. David Harris came to teach at the university for a semester in 1962. He came with his wife and their four-year-old daughter, Sarah (see fig. 9). Sarah had a nervous disposition, was fearful of the sound of police or ambulance sirens, and, in a strange town and country, strongly objected to the absence of her parents, even for a short time. I offered to babysit for the Harrises so that they could take in a movie. They assured me that they would let Sarah know that I, her playmate on many occasions, would keep her company. I arrived, Sarah was already in bed asleep, the Harrises left. An hour or so later, I heard the siren—a distant sound that grew louder and louder as the car approached. It woke up Sarah, who rushed into the living room expecting her parents but found me. She recognized me. She did not at all care for what she saw. Her face puckered in revulsion and she howled.

Among my worst nightmares is to give offense, like Frankenstein's monster, by my physical appearance alone. The nightmare need not be actual; it can occur when I am already awake. For example, when I wake up in the middle of the night, feeling unwell, I say to myself, Suppose I were to die in my sleep, who will discover my body? Worse, when? The question of when is especially urgent in summer, for there are no classes then and no one will expect to see me at the office. A maid comes in to clean my apartment every other week. Will she be the one to discover my body? Anxiety builds up, threatening to turn into panic unless I quickly get out of bed, for I see no way out of a scenario that, even if it is not realized this time, may well be realized the next. In an actual nightmare I have indeed died in my sleep. My room turns hot. My body starts to decompose. I wait and wait for someone to find me. I hear, at last, a scratch at the door. The maid is coming in. I jump out of bed to warn her—but wait! What can be worse than to be greeted by a gesticulating corpse?

In chapter 2, I said that, unlike most people's, my life is a shift from the public world of childhood to the private world of adulthood. My growth, to put the same thought somewhat differently, is from cosmos to hearth rather than the other way round. I see another difference between me and other people. In Asian societies—particularly the Hindu but also the Chinese—it is expected that a man be passionate with the affairs of the flesh and of the world when he is young but that, as he ages and the blood cools, he turn increasingly to nature and find beauty and elation there. That isn't, however, my story. As a young man, I was very much engaged with the beauties of nature. After all, I was a geographer, and in youth I did fieldwork in both the deserts and the humid tropics. The flesh had its yearnings, but to an extraordinary degree the yearnings were subordinated to the charms and mysteries of the nonhuman earth.

When I was fifty, something happened—changes in body chemistry, no doubt. For from then on, the splendidly varied features of the earth—mountains and plains, towns and cities, quaint shops and soaring skyscrapers—no longer commanded my attention, except as things to think about. Even in my role as a professional geographer, my interest was to turn more and more to concepts and generalizations than to the particular and the unique. By late middle age, I no longer felt the urge to travel and see the world, for I *have* traveled and seen the world; not all of it, of course, but enough for me to say, What's the point of multiplying instances? Do I really need to see the Taj Mahal under moonlight or sunrise over the Himalayas? Will my life seem incomplete without such experiences? By late middle age, I had become (to my surprise) a Greek: that is to say, like Socrates and Plato, my passion was for the beauty of the extremes—the heavens at one

end and the human individual at the other—rather than for the loveli-
nesses of the middle range: society, landscape, and place.

Of course, Socrates would not have minced words: he would have
said "boy" rather than "human individual." Homoeroticism had a public
place in ancient Greek society. In our society, it does not and this despite the
considerable increase in legal rights for, and public acceptance of, people
drawn to members of their own gender. I strongly believe—and I know
that my position is unacceptable to gay politicians—that no matter how
enlightened society eventually becomes, same-sex love will continue to
seem *peculiar,* not only to society at large but to its practitioners. Perhaps
all persecuted (or once persecuted) minority peoples feel irremediably
peculiar, and a little uncomfortable, if only because all, each in their own
way, continue to see themselves as an exception (but not an admired exception) to the norm; it is belonging to the norm, or to an *admired* exception to
it (such as a military class), that enables people to feel natural and relaxed
and to behave without edgy defensiveness. Compared, however, with persons of minority culture, class, and race, those of same-sex love may feel
the most marginalized, with the least likelihood of total, unthinking acceptance in some utopian future, for they are up against not only a universal
fact of biology but a fact of biology that culture glamorizes in increasing
volume, with increasing skill and fervor.

Biologically, human beings are a species that couples to reproduce, and
their bodies are constructed in accordance with this imperative. Culturally,
a large majority of people in all times and places have celebrated heterosex
ual love and union. Millennial accumulations in works of art, music, and
literature, and (in modern times) movie and television drama have only one
basic message—the naturalness, the goodness, and the beauty of a Romeo
embracing a Juliet. How can a male who loves another male read the following heterosexual paean by John Updike without a sense of exclusion, a
tinge of sadness, a wish to protest while knowing that to protest is somehow always to protest too much?

Watching the Olympic Games ice-dancing the other night on television, I was
struck by the primordial poetry of a man and woman together—each sex with its
different fleshly center of emphasis and style of contour, each with its special biological assignment and evolved social expectations, but partnered, mutually com-
pensatory, supportive and amusing and excitingly, maddeningly strange to each
other, together making a single species. As the couples flashed and glided over the
ice, intertwining, some sweet brute truth hulked dimly out of animal past, from
near where sex was invented by the algae and ferns, and I wanted to cry in joy,
feeling humanity, mine and the ice-dancers', as a spot of warmth within vast dark
coldness.[11]

As a schoolboy in Australia, I was drawn to another boy. But no alarm bell rang, for other boys, especially the older ones, were also drawn to him. I still remember this schoolmate. He was somewhat younger than most of us and looked delicate without being effeminate. He had a small well-shaped mouth that was always slightly open, warm peach-colored cheeks, large eyes topped by long lashes, and a crown of unruly fair hair. But my feeling toward another boy, an athlete with the sleek beauty of a well-oiled machine, was another matter. I couldn't persuade myself even then that it was just displaced longing for female loveliness. One day he came to my desk. We talked a bit. He showed me the palm of his hand and asked me to press mine against his, which I did. He said, quite simply, that my hand was smaller and had the delicacy of a girl's. We left it at that. There was no name calling, no propositioning, no bullying. When, in 1946, my father was transferred to his new post in Manila, I insisted on joining him with my mother and sister. Unlike my two brothers, I didn't want to remain behind in Australia as a boarder in an all-male school. I didn't have the words to explain why, but it was a foreboding that in that environment I might yield to temptation or to force (or both)—the exact nature of which I feared to imagine—that would destroy me. I was then fifteen (see fig. 11).

Men have always looked at women longingly, lasciviously, or just admiringly. In Western society, men (and women too) freely comment on female beauty. The reverse is not true, though with sexual liberation girls may now court boys without coyness, and women may yet un-self-consciously compliment men on their physical appeal. In the privacy of the written word, however, women have always been less reticent. Social convention or no social convention, it is, after all, a woman's biological right to be drawn to the male sex and say so. I have always envied them this right. "Across the aisle from me [in a Greyhound bus] I suddenly noticed the most beautiful young man I had ever seen, sound asleep," writes Alice Adams. "A golden boy: gold hair and tawny skin, large beautiful hands spread loosely on his knees, long careless legs in soft washed-out jeans. I hardly dared look at him; some intensity in my regard might have wakened him, and then on my face he would have seen—not lust, it wasn't that, just a vast and objectless regard for his perfection, as though he were sculptured in bronze or gold."[12]

One reason that I keep reading, one after another, the female author Ellis Peters's Brother Cadfael mystery stories is that invariably they include a bold and gallant boy or young man as hero. Cadfael's illegitimate son is described in one novel as "clean-boned, olive skinned, fiercely beautiful."[13] In another Cadfael novel, written when Peters was more than seventy years old, she put herself in the position of an elderly female character

Fig. 11. My mother, my sister, and me in Manila, 1946. I was at an age when I couldn't stand the idea of being a boarder in an all-male school.

observing secretly an eighteen-year-old who was squire to a knight. The boy stood before the central fire on its flagged hearth. "He still had Andamar's cloak over his arm, the capuchon dangling from one hand. The light from the reviving flames gilded his stooping face into gold, smooth-cheeked, with elegant bones . . . and on his dreaming lips the softest and most beguiling of smiles bore witness to his deep happiness. His flaxen hair swung against his cheek, and parted above the suave nape of his neck, the most revealing beauty of the young."[14]

And here is Helen Keller's rhapsody. She was blind, but to compensate she had an acute—a poetic—sense of smell. "Masculine exhalations are, as a rule, stronger, more vivid, more widely differentiated than those of women. In the odor of young men there is something elemental, as of fire, storm, and salt sea. It pulsates with buoyancy and desire. It suggests all the things strong and beautiful and joyous and gives me a sense of physical happiness."[15] And here is Dorothy Day's glorious declaration of a woman's love that engages her mind as well as all her senses. "I loved him in every way, as a wife, as a mother even. I loved him for all he knew and pitied him for all he didn't know. I loved him for the odds and ends I had to fish out of his sweater pockets and for the sand and shells he brought in with his fishing. I loved his lean cold body as he got into bed smelling of the sea, and I loved his integrity and stubborn pride."[16]

Alexander von Humboldt died in 1859, ninety years old and a lifelong bachelor. In 1959 I was in Panama City, listening to a public lecture on Humboldt that marked the centenary of his death. In 1996 UCLA's department of geography asked me to give a talk that would inaugurate a lecture series named after Humboldt. I was most happy to oblige if only because preparing for the lecture would provide me with an excuse to revisit one of my heroes. Alexander von Humboldt was a hero to me for obvious reasons. He was a founder of modern physical geography, and I started my career as a physical geographer. He made remarkable contributions to the history of geographical exploration and was among the first to use landscape painting and poetry to extend the range of geographical experience—feeling, emotion, and concept—and these are the areas that make up humanistic geography, the intellectual focus of my mature years. I admired Humboldt also for his vitality. There it is again—vitality—the one quality necessary to high achievement that I conspicuously lack. As a young man, Humboldt's expeditions into tropical South America were on a heroic scale, but his energies barely waned even at age sixty, when he traveled twelve thousand miles over the wilds of Siberia and Central Asia in pursuit of new scientific knowledge.

But something else about Humboldt captured my attention. Why didn't he marry? He was eminently eligible—handsome, intelligent, a famous scientist, a nobleman. Moreover, he was by no means misanthropic: he enjoyed society and frequented salons when he was in Paris. He had numerous female admirers, whose company—one would have thought—could cure the loneliness he felt when he was not on the road or writing. The answer lay in his character. "Alexander will never be inspired by anything that does not come through men. Time, I believe, will tell that I am right," wrote Caroline to her new husband, Wilhelm von Humboldt, Alexander's older brother by two years. Alexander was then twenty-one and sometimes teased his sister-in-law by claiming to love a female jeweler forty years his senior who would love him for the polish of his nose! But Caroline was not fooled. Alexander's love was for men. The shy recipients of Alexander's letters hid the degree of their ardor, as did modern scholarship in its reluctance to tarnish the reputation of a world scientific figure—

the "last universal man," in the words of the eminent historian Hugh Trevor-Roper.

Alexander von Humboldt suffered (there is no other word for it) at least three profound entanglements of the heart. The first struck when Humboldt was a teenager and the beloved—Wilhelm Gabriel Wegener— was another teenager, a theology student. They were inseparable. When circumstance forced them to separate, Humboldt wrote letter after letter, filled with aching desire and descriptions of dreams of union: "Since that February 13, as we swore eternal brotherly love to each other, I feel that none of my other acquaintances can give me what you have for me. . . . When I measure the longing with which I wait for news from you, I am certain that no friend could love another more than I love you." Humboldt sought to persuade his friend to take up the study of plants and minerals so that one day they could travel the world together.[17]

An even more emotionally charged affair occurred when Humboldt was twenty-five and already successful, both as an inspector of mines and in his scientific work. His beloved was four years younger, an obscure infantry subaltern called Reinhard von Haeften. When Haeften married in 1795, Humboldt hosted a large party as though he was the one pledging marriage vows. He then hung around the couple in Bayreuth for another year. Maintaining intimacy became more and more difficult. They couldn't always stay in the same town. On a cold day in January 1797, when Humboldt grew depressed by the thought that his friend would inevitably grow apart from him, he wrote the most moving, sexually passionate letter, of his life.

Two years have passed since we met, since your fate became mine. I still bless the day when you confided for the first time in me, telling me how soothing it was for you. I felt better in your company, and from that moment I was tied to you as by iron chains. Even if you must refuse me, treat me coldly with disdain, I should still want to be with you . . . Never would I cease to remain attached to you, and I can thank heaven that I was granted before my death the grand experience of knowing how much two human beings can mean to each other. With each day, my love and attachment for you increase. For two years I have known no other bliss on earth but your gaiety, your company, and the slightest expression of your contentment. My love for you is not just friendship, or brotherly love—it is veneration, childlike gratefulness, and devotion to your will as my most exalted law.[18]

The third attachment occurred in 1809 when forty-year-old Humboldt met a much younger man, a talented physicist by the name of François Arago. They shared a passion for science and liberal politics. In Humboldt's admiring eyes, his young friend was more original in the one and more daring in the other. Once more, Humboldt found himself in a submissive position. It was he, the world-renowned scientist, who had to wait or plead, he who was always touchingly grateful when a short letter arrived or when he could meet his friend briefly after an absence. No doubt, Arago was genuinely fond of Humboldt, but he lacked time to cultivate their friendship, for, in addition to his scientific work and political activities, he was also a devoted family man. Sadly for Humboldt, their priorities did not match. In old age, Humboldt continued to be intellectually vigorous, he continued to receive honors and to be treated with respect. It was in matters of affection that, increasingly, he had to be content with crumbs.[19]

I gave my lecture on Humboldt on February 7, 1997, without mentioning any of the "affairs of the heart"—an old-fashioned expression I use deliberately to suggest romance as well as sexual yearning. I didn't because I wanted to concentrate on Humboldt's contributions to geography, directly through his own research and voluminous writings and indirectly through, on the one hand, encouraging younger scientists and, on the other hand, promoting the study of nature in the scientific and political establishments of his time. But I couldn't resist saying near the end of the lecture that Alexander von Humboldt, for all his achievements and acclaim, lacked "one thing that ought to be every human being's birthright—namely, a beloved person to share cookies with before turning in to bed."[20]

Of course, I wasn't thinking of just Humboldt then. Nor do I now think of him, primarily, as I describe his affectional attachments. In this the story of my life, I am necessarily the centerpiece. If I do not detail my own attachments, it is because I wish to offer a psychologically accurate portrait of the total person that I am, not a confession or case history of particular parts, however emotionally charged they were for a time. I try to take a page from the poets, who tell us that to capture a mood, a feeling, an intimate or sublime experience, one must resort to the technique of indirection. I resort to indirection for another reason. It puts a distance between me and my loves that seems to me just right, for there *is* that distance, even in my most aching desire for the warmth of another human being's body. Why this distance? The short answer is to say, again, that I am less a Chinese than a Greek. And to a Greek of the fifth century B.C., yes, there is the beauty of youth. But there is also the beauty—the greater allure—of the cosmos.

Without the cosmos, without, more precisely, my delight in the harmonies of nature and of human works at their best, my life would be miserable—unlivable. I am saved by geography. Naturally, I see harshness and ugliness in the world "out there," as I do in my disordered interior world. I even believe that my own misery, my unalterably subaltern status in society for all the outward shows of acceptance, gives me an insight into human misery and especially into what it means to belong to a disdained minority group. However, I choose not to dwell in the shadows—my own or the world's. Have I gone too far in the opposite direction—have I too often dwelled in the beauties of the cosmos? Am I an escapist, or am I, to put myself in the best possible light, not only expressing an important side of my own nature, which happens to be optimistic, but also reminding the erudite world, occupationally prone to seeing the dark side of things, that there also exist the beautiful and the good? I don't know. How can anyone know?

5

Salvation by Geography

IN OCTOBER 1951 I left home—Paris—for Berkeley, where I was to be a graduate student. Throughout the summer of that year I had been sick—my stomach churned constantly, I had no appetite, and I could barely retain the little I ate. I consulted several physicians and went to the American Hospital for a thorough check-up. They could find nothing wrong. It was all in my mind. I was an immature and pampered twenty-year-old, and the prospect of being entirely on my own in a new country an ocean and a continent away from parental undergirding unnerved me (see fig. 12). But, of course, I couldn't and didn't admit it. At New York harbor, where the ship docked, I sent home a telegram to inform my parents of my safe arrival, as had been agreed upon, but added, "I am happy to be here." What a liar! I couldn't have been more miserable, and yet I had to say "I am happy" to give myself encouragement, and it worked. I did feel better.

I crossed the continent by train. It was still the way to travel in those days. I have no memory at all of the journey from New York to Chicago, but the next stage of the journey, from Chicago to Berkeley in a newer train—one that boasted a Vistadome—was a revelation. I had read about the Great Plains and the Rocky Mountains as a geography student in England, but book learning did not prepare me for the splendors of reality. As for the train itself, I appreciated the amenities—the comfortable seats, the spaciousness, and the general cleanliness of the cars. But it was also in the train that I encountered unfair treatment among strangers for the first time.

Around noon, just when I was feeling the pleasant gnawings of hunger, the steward walked the corridors, ringing a bell to announce that lunch was being served. Many cars separated me from the diner. By the time I reached it, all the tables were occupied, and a long line had formed. The steward came to the line periodically to call out passengers in groups

Fig. 12. Graduation from Oxford, June 1951. An immature twenty-year-old looked forward to graduate work at Berkeley.

of two, three, or four, so that they could be seated together in the vacated places. Fair enough. But when he started to select, repeatedly, a single passenger from behind me and seated him or her first, I knew that I was being discriminated against, no doubt because I looked impecunious and it paid him to give preferential treatment to more affluent passengers. I had to repress my anger, for the steward was all-powerful and I did not have the choice of going elsewhere. Strange to think that, at the time, I failed to see race—the steward was black, I was yellow, and the other passengers were white—as perhaps the single most important cause of discrimination.

I recognized racial bias when other people were targeted, as the black maids were at International House in Chicago. But I was blind when it was directed at me. That I might be ignored for no other reason than the color of my skin simply did not register. All this changed from the 1970s on-ward. Thanks to a nationwide movement to raise consciousness in regard to the color of one's skin, I am now—white friends, beware!—on guard for every slur or slight. Whether this constitutes an improvement in the direction of greater social harmony and personal happiness, I do not know. I rather doubt it.

To continue with my story, after two days on the road, across the great open spaces of America, so liberating compared with the tight little land-scapes of England, the train pulled into Berkeley. As soon as I settled down, I went to see my adviser, John Kesseli, a German Swiss geographer. I was ignorant of California custom and put on a coat and a tie for the occasion. Almost the first thing Kesseli said to me was: "You don't really want to study geography. I know Chinese students. They come to Califor-nia for the sun. If they work for an advanced degree, it is so that they can return home and land a cushy job." There was a pause. Then he continued at an even more personal level. "You want to be a geomorphologist? But look at you now [he was no doubt referring to my coat and tie], you are not the sort to do serious fieldwork, you are not the sort to get dirt under your fingernails." I was stunned. I went to my fellow students for advice and consolation. One of them—an older grad (Tom Pagenhart)—had his feet on the table. He listened to my story and said: "Well, never mind. Kesseli has a rough exterior, but once you get to know him, you will find that he has a heart of—stone." Stone! How well I remember that elegant pause before the thunderbolt. I appreciated the wit. Despite my forebod-ing, I knew I was all right—that I had come to the right place. And I need hardly add that the cliché held true: under the rough exterior, Kesseli had a heart of gold.

I was happy at Berkeley. My intellectual horizon opened up as it never had before. I was only fifteen when I chose geography as my field. Twelve years later, in 1957, I received my doctoral degree. So ended my long period of formal training. Ever since, I have not only taught and done research in geography but I have breathed and lived it. How was (is) that possible? How can geography, a rather down-to-earth subject, have such a hold on me, offer me "salvation" when, from time to time, my personal life seemed to be the pits? I couldn't have answered properly as a teenager or even as a newly minted Ph.D. I can give a well-rounded answer only late in life—in retrospect, for the meaning of geography has expanded over a lifetime. It grew as I grew.

My vocation in geography can be baffling to colleagues in other disciplines. At faculty socials, I have been asked, "Why are you a geographer, or why do you call yourself one?" It is a strange question, for I can't imagine a historian or a political scientist being so queried. Perhaps my unimposing physical appearance prompts it, for people even now tend to see the geographer as a robust explorer in the mold of Robert Falcon Scott or Indiana Jones. As a matter of fact, when I was an undergraduate, the professors of geography at both Oxford and Cambridge were explorers. The question may also have been prompted by the titles I have given to some of my books. People don't immediately understand how *Morality and Imagination, Passing Strange and Wonderful, Cosmos and Hearth,* and *Escapism* can be the works of a geographer.[1]

To those who have wondered about my vocation, I respond in three ways, each geared to a different level of seriousness. At a social gathering, when people are not at their most attentive, I am likely to say, "As a child, I moved around a great deal with my family, and there is nothing like travel to stimulate one's appetite for geography." Sad to say, this lazy answer nearly always suffices, for it is what my inquirer expects. My second and more thoughtful response is "I have always had an inordinate fear of losing my way. Of course, no one likes to be lost, but my dread of it is excessive. I suspect that more than physical discomfort is at stake. To be lost is to be paralyzed, there being no reason to move one way rather than another. Even back and front cease to be meaningful. Life, with no sense of direction, is drained of purpose. So, even as a child, I concluded that I had to be a geographer so as to ensure that I should never be disoriented." Geographers, I assumed, always knew where they were. They always had a map somewhere—either in their backpack or in their head.

A childhood hero of mine was Sherlock Holmes. I admired him and considered him a superb geographer because he could always find his way, whether in the back streets of London and Chicago or in the wilds of

Utah and Tibet. Moreover, Holmes was always socially at ease: he knew how to behave, whether the venue was a duchess's drawing room, a Mormon meeting hall, or an opium den. That too I found most admirable for, like most young people, I feared social disorientation quite as much as I did the geographical kind. This fear of losing my way has strongly affected my environmental preferences. Unlike many people, I prefer American towns with their geometric street patterns to Old World towns with their maze of narrow alleys. Old World towns are unfriendly to strangers, who must stay a long time to feel spatially comfortable. By contrast, the open grid characteristic of many American towns says right away, "Welcome, stranger." I dislike the tropical rainforest for the same reason: unless one is a native, it invites disorientation. I like the desert because it is an open map, with the sun serving as a dependable marker of east and west, and with sharply etched landforms—visible from miles away—that unmistakably tell visitors where they are.

But my dread of rainforest and love of desert hint at something deeper than just orientation. Beneath such likes and dislikes are questions of one's fundamental attitude toward life and death. In the rainforest, all I can see and smell—perversely, I admit—is decay. In the desert, by contrast, I see not lifelessness but purity. I sometimes say teasingly to environmentalists that, unlike them, I am a genuine lover of nature. But by "nature" I mean the planet Earth, not just its veneer of life—and the whole universe, which is overwhelmingly inorganic.

This leads to my most serious reply to the question, "Why are you a geographer?" I took up geography because I have always wondered, perhaps to a neurotic degree, about the meaning of existence: I want to know what we are doing here, what we want out of life. Yes, but why geography? Surely it is much more sensible to seek insight in religious studies or philosophy? My answer takes up the remainder of this chapter. It is personal, as is appropriate in an autobiography, but it will also show how geography can be taken in directions that even well-informed people (academic geographers, among them) do not venture. The downside to following a different path is that it has made me an oddity in a discipline that I have considered my home for more than fifty years.

So, back to the big woozy questions concerning the meaning of existence, what we really want out of life. Children on the verge of puberty commonly raise them and then pass on to life's more immediate and practical challenges. I differ in that I haven't been able to do so. They haunt me even now in old age. Why is this? Why can't I put the unanswerables behind me as others have? I suspect that my enthrallment is an effect of something inborn, such that a troublesome event or experience that most people can shrug off lingers to whip me into ceaseless, often tiring, sometimes exhilarating, effort. Consider death, not only in the world "out there," but as personal fate. Children confront it at some stage and then blessedly forget. I, by contrast, can't shake the nightmarish logic with which my own mortality first impressed itself on me. I was twelve. In my first and only philosophical dream, I saw that my being alive had one absolutely certain corollary, which was that I would die. Struggling vainly to be free of the logic was the nightmare. Relief came when I realized that I was dreaming and that the reality of day would deliver me. But of course it didn't. Quite the contrary. Fully awake, I had to fully accept that I was indeed alive; the awful consequence—death—therefore remained.

I now see more clearly than ever why the desert had such profound appeal. I was drawn not only to its pure lines and ease of orientation but to barrenness itself—to a presentation of absence that enabled me to wipe out in one clean sweep sex, biological life, and death. By contrast, the rain forest forced me to confront choking growths and struggle, rubbed my nose in the pungent odor of decay, which fused in my mind with the pungent odor of sex.

But I had another reason for my dislike of the rainforest—its threat to individuality. Death, of course, means the end of individuality and reabsorption into an undifferentiated whole. But the rainforest denies individuality in its very superfluity of life. In the dense biomass, no single plant, animal, or human being can stand out. By contrast, in the desert, every living thing is proudly itself, separated by space from other living things. In the desert, I felt almost too conspicuous, a lone rod casting a sharply edged shadow on the floor. On those occasions when I encountered another human being, I saw him, unique and precious, in beautiful clarity against a vast backdrop of sand and sky.

Throughout childhood, youth, and young adulthood, I have had to wrestle with my individuality—my apartness from others—which stirred in me conflicting emotions of pride and anguish. Just who was I behind my socially approved roles? Subtly denigrated for being thin-skinned as a child, I became even more self-conscious, more aware of my difference from other children, with sexual awakening. Why did I not enjoy the rough tumble of other boys? Why was I unable to get the point of their sexual jokes? Oxford's all-male college exacerbated my feelings of isolation and difference. For the good of the college, I agreed to be coxswain, only to wonder why an undersized Chinese was seated at one end of the boat, barking commands at eight burly Englishmen (see fig. 13).

At U.C.–Berkeley, my adviser called me "an Englishman with a Chi-

Fig. 13. An Oxford Eight rowing boat on the Thames, with me as coxswain. The year was probably 1949.

nese face." He rather liked his coinage and used it frequently. So it was announced to the world that I wore a mask. But the mask did not hide an Englishman or any other respectable, acculturated human being. If only it were so! My fellow students, I felt enviously, had no need of masks, being all of a piece, with about them a New World—a California—wholesomeness, a firm grounding in culture and society, a natural manner of speaking about football and girls, that I not only did not have but could never have. I yearned to communicate with these Americans, but it seemed that the only way I could do so was through the feints and thrusts of social talk or the technical language of geography.

Given so many opportunities for introspection, for pondering the sort of person I am, it is almost inevitable that I should one day want to try my hand at autobiography. Years ago, I had already begun to prepare myself for the task—although I didn't know it at the time—by writing a book that addressed questions of community and self, shared identity and individuality, at an impersonal level. The book is called *Segmented Worlds and Self: Group Life and Individual Consciousness* (1982). Let me give a brief account of its making and central thesis.

Self-consciousness is a uniquely human trait. How is it related to the development of individuality and the need for privacy? How would an individual's growing sense of self affect social cohesion and group life? It is a topic of natural appeal to the geographer, for a heightening of self-consciousness and individuality clearly evolved with the progressive partitioning of space. Partitioned space promotes privacy by allowing individuals to be alone, engage in separate activities, have separate thoughts, or explore each other's world in sustained conversation. To prepare for the book, I thought what I needed to do was refurbish and extend my knowledge of the European house from the Middle Ages to the late nineteenth century, concentrate on the number and arrangement of rooms, the purposes they served, and correlate these changes in spatial organization with the history of consciousness.

It seemed a worthwhile project. Yet after a year or two of reading and writing, I grew discouraged. I could see a decade of hard work ahead, in the course of which I would be wiser in details but not necessarily in understanding, for my arc of vision would have stayed essentially the same. Just as I was about to give up my project on specialized rooms and individuality, it suddenly occurred to me that the story could be given greater texture and far more resonance by placing it between two other narratives—one on food and eating, the other on the theater.

The medieval manor house was little more than its centerpiece—the hall, an unsegmented area in which all sorts of activities took place. Similarly, food eaten there was either a whole animal, a hefty shank, or a stew of many ingredients thrown together with little consideration for compatibility. Life in the Middle Ages was public and gregarious. Food was eaten heartily; table manners were minimal. People had few places to which they could withdraw, and they did not seem to mind. There was a strong sense of self but little self-consciousness.

Obviously, I cannot trace the delicately interwoven stories of house, food, and table manners here. But the essence of what I am getting at is clear enough. By the late nineteenth century, the great European house had probably reached a maximum degree of partitioning and specialization. A room existed for every purpose—including that of being alone with one's books and thoughts. Dining reached a height of refinement, not so much in flavor as in the quality and number of utensils. Meat in vulgar bulk, except for the roast in England, was banished from the table. Foods were served separately, not indiscriminately mixed as in the Middle Ages and even into the seventeenth century. To proper Victorians, dining was a ritual at which drinking a wine inappropriate to the meat, or confusing the fish knife with the butter knife, was an embarrassing breach of etiquette. Whereas in earlier times guests shared a bench at the dining table, now each guest was ensconced in his own chair and had before him his own private world of sparkling glasses and silverware. He was expected to eat as if nothing so gross as nourishment had crossed his mind, and as if the real purpose for sitting down to table was to engage in polite conversation with his charming neighbors.

More exciting and potentially more revealing than the story of food and eating is the story of the theater. Social scientists seek models of society and yet have curiously neglected the theater as model. The theater is a model both in its sociospatial organization and in the plays enacted on its stage. Again, I am able to offer only a few pointers here. As physical space, the medieval theater was, like the church building, a cosmos, embracing heaven, earth, and underworld. In the market square, where plays were periodically performed, actors and spectators freely intermingled; no proscenium arch and curtain, no lighted stage and darkened hall (all much later inventions) separated them.

The sort of promiscuous mixing I noted in the medieval hall and in medieval cooking was also a feature of the medieval theater. As for the play's theme, what could it be other than the salvation of man? Plays were morality plays. Even those of a much later time—Shakespeare's, for example—might still be considered morality plays, with the scope and trappings of the medieval worldview still lingering about them, if only because of their cosmic resonance and religious underpinning and their performance in an all-embracing space called the Globe. How strikingly different the theater became in the eighteenth and nineteenth centuries when, rather than the cosmos, there was landscape, a much more subjective concept, and the human drama of cues and miscues, failed communication, and loneliness eventually moved to interior space—the living room. Late nineteenth-century plays that depict individual separateness within rooted, communal life find a parallel in the theater's own physical arrangement—its compartmentalized spaces. Actors and spectators do not mix. The sense of one world—the Globe—is missing. On the one side is the illuminated stage, on the other, the darkened hall in which spectators sit in their separate chairs, as if alone.

In *Segmented Worlds and Self* I also examined other cases of human individuation and the circumstances that promoted them: for example, the well-known contrast in the tightness of social bonding between premodern communities and modern societies. The word *society* itself gained currency over *community* from the sixteenth century onward to suggest a less adhesive, more contractual human relationship. *We* was the dominant, almost exclusive pronoun in earlier times, with *I* used increasingly (likewise, the mirror) in Europe from, again, the sixteenth century onward.

I noted the shifting emphasis in the use of the senses. Proximate senses—those of touch and odor, especially—encouraged bonding, the loss of self in a greater whole. Before, say, 1600, Europeans, like peoples of simple culture even in the twentieth century, touched and caressed one another often, slept nonsexually with friends or strangers, and were remarkably tolerant of bad odor. In modern times, by contrast, touch tends to be regarded as an invasion of personal space, unwelcome except in desired sexual congress, and odor—diffuse and all-enveloping—as primitive, intellectually disreputable. Smell has come to connote smelly; odor is almost always construed to mean bad odor, with the result that both human beings and places aspire to be as odorless as possible. The sense that has found increasing favor since the onset of the early modern period is sight. Far more than the other senses, it opens up the world, giving its objects definition and vividness. That property and the lingering image of God's all-seeing and all-comprehending eye incline one to regard sight as providing an objective view of the world. On the other hand, sight also pulls the other way—toward subjectivism, the position that how the world looks depends on where one stands. In the late twentieth century, the trend is from the idea of an all-encompassing visual space shared by all to individual points of view, each different from the other. Sight, thus understood and used, is both symptomatic of and contributary toward the change from community to isolated selves.

An area that I failed to consider in *Segmented Worlds and Self* is the role of language in group bonding and in the making of individuals. How can language do both? How can it both bind and separate? Since writing the book, two events have led me to ponder these questions. One is the alarm about the rapid disappearance of languages: scores become extinct every year. And because language is intimately tied to culture or form of life, the loss is also a loss of cultural diversity.[2] Anthropologists' attitudes toward such diminishment are rather like those of a museum curator. The world's languages and cultures are their charge; their range and number are a measure of the museum's wealth and prestige. Every loss is therefore to be regretted. Moreover, the loss is not only a marriage custom here, an unusual way of making pots there, but also, at a more general level, an intense type of bonding. Intense bonding is an effect of sharing customs and practices, but, above all, of sharing a language that may be incomprehensible even to neighboring groups of similar culture.

The second event that has prompted me to think about language is more personal. As a young geographer, I felt very much a part of a group. Somewhere along the path to intellectual maturity, I lost that warm feeling of belonging. What happened? I blame language—my expanding vocabulary, greater command over syntax, and an enhanced power of thinking—for my increased sense of isolation.

For speech to bind rather than isolate, the conversational vocabulary has to be limited, as it almost invariably is. Even when people talk a lot, they say little. Language is more a device for reassuring group members that they belong than one of gaining knowledge and opening up the world. Suppose someone does see language as first and foremost a tool of understanding. In time, he will build an imposing edifice of knowledge, but he may have to pay the price of becoming a prisoner in it, isolated from his colleagues.

Let me pursue the architectural metaphor. Consider a university, where—if anywhere—language specialization and expansion are encouraged. In such a place, graduate students live in sparsely furnished rooms but share a house—the intellectual house of Marx, Gramsci, Foucault, or whoever the favored thinker happens to be. A warm sense of community develops as the students encounter one another in the hallways and speak a common language, with passwords such as capital formation, hegemony, and the theater of power to establish firmly their corporate membership. Time passes. As the students mature intellectually, they move from the shared life of a house to rented apartments scattered in the same neighborhood. The apartments are close enough that friends still feel free to drop in for visits, and when they do the entire living space is filled with talk and laughter, recapturing as in younger days not only the bonhomie but also the tendency to embrace wholeheartedly the currently fashionable doctrine. Eventually, the students become professors themselves. They begin modestly to build their own house of intellect and add to the structure as they prosper. Because each house bears witness to a scholar's achievement, it can be a source of great personal satisfaction. But the downside is whether anyone will want to visit. And if a colleague or friend does, why should the person spend time in more than one room?

Social scientists assert that a tenement, where people hang out the wash or sit on the stoop to socialize, can be a very sympathetic, communal place. By contrast, a suburb with freestanding houses is cool and unfriendly. I am saying that the same may be true of intellectual life as one moves to larger houses of one's own design. Both types of move—socioeconomic and intellectual—signify success, and with both the cost to the mover may well be a sense of isolation and vulnerability. A scholar who has achieved a distinctive style that makes his work an easy target for criticism or outright dismissal may look back nostalgically to an earlier time when neither his thought nor his style stood out, when he lived inconspicuously and communally with others in an intellectual edifice constructed by someone else.[3]

Consciousness of being an individual, with its satisfactions and pain, was a strong motivation for writing books such as *Segmented World and Self* (1982) and *Cosmos and Hearth* (1996). What, one might ask, motivated me to write *Dominance and Affection: The Making of Pets* (1984)? I can't identify all the forces at work but one that I can is a sadomasochistic streak in my make-up, which I mentioned earlier. Most people have such a streak; it is no cause for shame unless it becomes virulent. Most people, for example, enjoy dominating and toying with another. We have animal pets, in part, for that reason. A sense of power, tinged with eroticism, pleasantly massages our ego when we command a dog to sit, roll over, or fetch. Both the sense of power and the eroticism are far greater when we can command a human being to "roll over"—well, no, that would be excessive—but "fetch"? Don't we issue this order to our subordinates, more or less nicely, all the time? As for masochism, there is a touch of it in all of us—a residuum of the delicious passivity of early childhood when a parent is in total control. And it is reinforced by the grail of total submission—the ecstasy of self loss—in sexual congress.

The mild sadomasochistic tendency in all of us may have gone a step further in me, especially at the masochistic end of the continuum. Rather than turn inward to tame the impulse, I fight it by making use of it, treating it as evidence and a source of insight concerning the external world. How, I ask, is sadomasochism manifested in society, especially in respectable society? What does its prevalence say about human nature? *Dominance and Affection* is my tentative answer. The book may seem to deviate sharply from the traditional themes of geography, but this is not so. It belongs with geography—even with mainstream geography. What makes the book different is its twist. But before I can explain what that is, I must first say something about the mainstream.

There are several mainstreams in human geography, several historically rooted, broadly accepted approaches, one of which is studying how humans have transformed the earth. This particular approach received a major impetus in 1955, when three distinguished scholars, Carl Sauer, Marston Bates, and Lewis Mumford, organized an international symposium to demonstrate its fruitfulness and a further impetus when the different interpretations were published in a much acclaimed volume called *Man's Role in Changing the Face of the Earth*. I was a student at Berkeley in the early fifties, which were also Carl Sauer's last years before retirement. I could sense the excitement—the importance of what was going on. Since the sixties, this flurry of excitement on university campuses has become the well-organized, sometimes well-financed, often passionate, global environmental movement. Publications quickly reached floodtide.

Overwhelmingly, they emphasized, as they still do, how human economic activities, driven by necessity and even more by greed, have drastically altered and all too often despoiled the earth.

Dominance and Affection is mainstream insofar as it too can be taken as a study of how humans have transformed the earth. But, as the title indicates, the book's point of departure is psychological rather than economic, and its concern is more with human nature than with nature "out there." That's the twist. I have shifted focus from economic to aesthetic exploitation, and by aesthetic exploitation I mean the mistreatment of nature, including human beings, for purposes of pleasure and art. I ask the reader to picture not cattle yoked to the plow or trees cut down to make houses but rather the toy poodle, the potted garden, and the pampered underlings of a potentate. In the last set of examples, power is applied to create comeliness and beauty and with a certain affection for the manipulated objects. Power so used tends to be regarded as benign, in part because it does not bring about massive, deleterious changes on the earth's surface. I cast a shadow on this attractive picture by saying that power can be even more uninhibited, more arbitrary and cruel, when it is playful.

Play is such a sunny word that we forget its dark side. It is bad to be "used," but it can be worse to be "played with." This observation, though a psychological truism, only penetrated my skull to fuel my research imagination when I read William Styron's fictionalized account of Nat Turner, the slave who led the only effective sustained revolt in the American South, in 1831. An old degenerate by the name of Eppes purchased Turner with the view of transforming him into a sexual pet, but economic greed changed Eppes's mind and Turner was made to toil in the fields instead. As the hero of the novel put it: "If I had become the compliant vessel of his cravings he might have found it much harder to run me until my legs felt like stumps."[4]

In *Dominance and Affection*, the first pet I introduce is water. It may seem poetic license to call water a pet, for a pet is normally thought of as animate, whereas water is decidedly not an organism. Yet, in the imagination, water is almost universally considered "alive." This moving and living force is harnessed for many economic ends, but it is also a plaything. We train it, we force it to act against its nature for our amusement, captivatingly, as fountains that leap and impart an air of spontaneous joy to the garden. There is nothing spontaneous about fountains, however, which are rather clear examples of submission to power. Their existence requires channeling water from distant sources through canals, tunnels, and aqueducts—a complex organization in which managers, engineers, skilled workers, and a large labor force must effectively cooperate. Moreover, the

Fig. 14. The massive fountains—the *fontana dell'organo idraulico*—devised by Orazio Olivieri for the Villa d'Este at Tivoli. (Drawing by Wayne Howell)

choreography of spouting water depends on the development of a sophisticated hydraulic science. From the sixteenth to the eighteenth century, fountains were among the most showy pets of European princes (see fig. 14).

Following this excursus into the playful use of water, I move on to the "petification" of plants and animals, and, in the process, tread—perhaps with rather a heavy foot—on the idea that the great or aesthetic garden can be considered as belonging to the sphere of nature and innocence. Backyard gardens might be so categorized but not the princely garden, which is as artificial and artifactual as the palatial house to which it is attached.

Indeed, my favorite image of the human domination of nature in preindustrial times is not monumental architecture but the aesthetic garden, especially the miniaturized kind known as *penjing* in Chinese and bonsai in Japanese. The bonsai is wilderness reduced to potted landscape, domesticated in the literal sense and by exquisite means of torture (*torture* in the literal sense of twisting and bending), sustained with loving attention to detail over an extended period of time.

Individualism, sadomasochism. And now I turn to aestheticism. Each is rooted in my nature and each has been a motor driving and directing a long-term writing project. Some kind of biological determinism would seem to be at work, which makes me unhappy. This is only natural if biology has dealt me a blank card—absence of mathematical talent, for example—or a joker—sick masochism, for example. But even when it has dealt me a fair card, I can still feel dissatisfaction, perversely desiring something else. An aesthetic temperament is, to me, such a fair card. For as long as I can remember, I have appreciated beauty in things—the color of a marble, the shape of a toy truck, beauty in nature if it is crystalline, and human beauty. But I rebelled. I didn't want to be an aesthete. That I, with my slender build, might look like one—and body build is biological destiny—added to my resentment. And so I dressed to keep warm and to be unnoticed, and I have never spent time thinking how my home might be decorated to advantage. The only work of art that I have ever purchased for myself isn't even a work of art—it is a Tiffany apple. Too much concern with pleasing surfaces and appearances was and is a temptation that I have sought to resist.

Nevertheless, looking back, I can see how the aesthetic point of view has made its way into such works as *Topophilia* (1974), *The Good Life* (1986), and *Passing Strange and Wonderful* (1993)—as an undercurrent in the first two books and openly in the third, which is subtitled *Aesthetics, Nature, and Culture.* What made me come out of the closet and embrace aestheticism? It was the realization, embarrassingly late in life, that the root meaning of aestheticism and the aesthetic is 'feeling'. To feel is to come to life—to be alive. Aesthesia (esthesia) or aesthesis is coming to life, as its opposite—anaesthesia—is closing down life, a deadening of the senses. And there is nothing superficial about coming to life, drawn by the beauties of the world and wanting to add to them. Isn't human culture—everything from the well-turned phrase to great systems of thought, from cosmetized hair to great works of architecture—a striving toward a keener, more shapely, more comprehensive and comprehensible life?

I argued this point of view in 1990 with an architect at the Detroit International Airport. We were both on our way to Toronto to attend the annual meeting of the Association of American Geographers and ran into each other at a fast-food stand. Carrying on a conversation was difficult, for the stand provided no place to sit. He looked annoyed and complained to me about the disappearance of full-service restaurants in airports and the general decline of architectural standard. I sympathized and said I knew just what he meant. Yet, I added, "Let us not allow the chase after the big buck in commercialism to overwhelm altogether the fact that everything we see here is also a striving toward comeliness. Just look at the plastic soup bowl that I am about to discard. Why waste time and money on a decorated rim? Maybe my judgment is warped by having entered my second childhood, but I am inclined to find an admirable aesthetic impulse in every humanly made object, even in this cruddy place. Take paper napkins. At one time I would have said, 'Where is the linen?' Now I say, 'How artfully folded!'"

The book *Space and Place: The Perspective of Experience* was published in 1977. Its genesis lay in a course of the same title that I taught for the first time in 1973 and continued to teach every other year until I did it for the last time in the fall semester of 1997. Naturally, in this twenty-five-year period, I expanded some themes and curtailed others, abandoned old ones to make room for the new. I can't help noticing that the general drift in the lectures was in the direction of aesthetics and space. As for place, even in the book I tended to give a once-over-lightly to family, home, rootedness, and heritage—just when these institutions and the past were finding renewed favor with the American public—just when, in other words, "Fence me in" was elbowing out the earlier (and my preferred) slogan, "Don't fence me in." I praised "place," but my contribution to the understanding of place was not so much in the rhetoric of rootedness, already beginning to flood both academic and popular literature, as in expanding its meaning.

I expanded place's meaning in two ways. One was to argue that *place*, defined broadly as a center of meaning (care and nurture), includes far more entities than towns and cities, or even neighborhoods, homes, and houses. Why not also fireplace, a favorite armchair, and even another human being—mother, for example, who is home to the toddler, a place to return to after playing in the sandlot? The second expansion was to say that place need not be rooted in locality, a common assumption. How can one deny that the great ship moving majestically across the ocean is a place—a sharply bounded world with the captain as priest-king? Mother is a place and, of course, mother moves. And, then, what about portable culture? for not all culture is anchored in locality. Consider classical music. It is home—a profound source of emotional support—to the music lover. When Bruno Walter migrated to the United States in 1938, he was asked whether he ever felt homesick for Germany, his native country, or for Austria, where he had last served as a symphony conductor. His reply was no, that music was his home—in the scores, which he could carry with him anywhere, in the orchestra, and, above all, in the performance itself.

But it was space that stirred my imagination and continues to do so. *Space,* historically and for most people in different parts of the world, has had a predominantly negative meaning. The word denotes openness and the danger that goes with such openness. I find it suggestive that the root meaning of "bad" is "to be wide open"—to be exposed to external influences, most of which, in older days, were considered threatening or evil. America's big appeal for me is that it has chosen to emphasize the positive meanings of space. Space connotes mobility, action, freedom, potentiality, the future. It connotes life, the sensation of coming to life. It is aesthesia. One reason that I am able to find a lilt in the human story is the progress that I can so clearly see in the human experience of movement and space, that is, of life.

The gist of this story is simple enough. Motion? A newborn shows what it can do by kicking its legs; an older infant by crawling; a child by standing up (defying gravity), walking, and running. Technology extends the biological repertoire. A child racing down a hill on his mountain bike feels speed and air, confident abandon, and joy. A man, revving up the engine of his motorcycle on an open stretch of a California highway through a landscape made surreal by fog, rushes into abstract space and buffeting wind. A pilot encased in a small airplane may seem at first blush isolated "from the great problems of nature, [but it] actually plunges him more deeply into them," says Antoine de Saint-Exupéry.[5]

Now, consider throwing objects into space as a means of extending the body's borders. What enormous progress humans have made! from spear tossed by a strong arm and arrow propelled by a taut bow to projectiles driven by explosives—cannon ball, bullet, rocket, missile, and the spacecraft *Pioneer 10,* which by 1996 had been "thrown" to a point 2.5 billion miles beyond the outer edge of the solar system.[6] It may still be there, beeping, when the sun turns into a red giant, swallowing up all its satellites except for the manmade one that has escaped. If life is motion, and motion the overcoming of inertia and gravity, *Pioneer 10* is a powerful symbol of life—of human intelligence that is never quite content with being in place.

Research has shown that unless we can move our limbs and move about, our appreciation of space through the eyes is minimal. But given the ability to move, the eyes (and ears too) add immensely to the subtlety, intensity, and scope of spatial experience. An aspect of space known to all human beings is the difference between inside and outside, interior and exterior. What is more fundamental than that? Yet the quality of "insideness," of interior space, varies enormously with the level of cultural accomplishment. The first big step forward was the controlled use of fire, which might have occurred about 200,000 years ago, that enabled our remote ancestors to live safely in caves by keeping dangerous animals out. The lived-in cave gave early humans, for the first time, a feeling for enclosed volume—a homey interior illuminated by fire throwing flickering light and shadow on the walls and ceiling, a bounded interiority that must have heightened the awareness of an "outside" that was open, exposed, and dangerous yet inviting.

Living in a cave was the first big step forward. Many more steps, big and small, have been taken since. Together they add up to astonishing progress in how human beings have been able to come to life—to feel alive—in an interior. I invite students to imagine the kinds of interior space available to people in earlier times, beginning with ancient Egypt. The pyramid, I say, is an overpowering presence viewed from the outside and perhaps life enhancing for that reason. But inside? Inside are cramped passageways that lead to the pharaoh's burial chamber—to suffocating airless space and death. As to the mortuary temples that line the Nile, for all their monumentality and clarity from the outside, inside their closely packed pillars and gloom allow no real sense of volume. And the same was true even of Greek temples, so elegant and polished on the outside, but inside they were dark and only roughly finished, houses for the cult statues of deities and not at all for their worshipers.

A sweeping departure, according to Sigfried Giedion, came with the construction of Hadrian's Pantheon (A.D. 118–128). Attention turned from exterior to interior, from compact sculpture to hollowed-out space. The Pantheon was a large hemispherical dome (141 feet in diameter) that rested on a cylindrical drum. By comparison with the exterior, the interior was elegantly finished and of a sublime simplicity. An opening at the top of the dome—the oculus—allowed sunlight to stream through and sweep the bowl of the hollowed space in the course of the day. Whereas the Egyptian and even the Greek temples, in their interior darkness, suggested the earth, the womb, death, and the rather desperate hope of another life, the Pantheon stood for the well-illuminated celestial firmament such that to enter it was to be, in a sense, already in heaven in the company of the gods.[7]

A high point in the "Space and Place" class was the exploration, in imagination, of the Gothic cathedral—a major innovation in the history of European architecture, a strikingly new way for Europeans (and eventually humanity) to experience space. The Gothic style, according to Erwin Panofsky, was not only the pointed arch and the crossed-ribbed vault, which made the interior soar and the spirit lift in a manner that the Romanesque had already achieved, but also light. The Gothic cathedral was a palace of light.[8] Windows were enlarged so that the walls were more glass than stone. Sunbeams penetrated and were refracted in the stained glass that artisans deliberately enriched and thickened to bring about an effect of implosion. With its exterior a delicate stone tracery, its interior aglow in subdued colors, the cathedral was an enormous jewel box set in the midst of mud and raucous street life. To modern eyes, it could seem paradoxical that people in the age of faith should be so worldly, show such an open love of gems and precious metals. But then we would be forgetting their symbolic meaning, which far transcended mere wealth. Jewelers of the time deliberately rounded rather than faceted their precious stones so as to produce, as with stained glass, an impression of light coming from within—an inner light that symbolized the inner shining virtues of Christian saints. God himself is light, as is his son, sent to the world that "all men through him might believe." Both the dithyrambs to light in the Gospel According to John and the Gothic architecture of light made their dramatic entry into church life and ritual in the twelfth century.

Sound too plays a vital role in spatial experience. Each sound can generate a spatial atmosphere of its own. Think of a seagull shrieking as it drifts out to the ocean, a train whistling at night as it dashes across the prairie, footsteps tapping on pavement in the empty square, a cat mewing in the alley, the subdued roar of traffic along a highway that runs through sun-drenched countryside. Again, in class, I lingered over the cathedral and expatiated at some length on the role of sound—everything from the single cough that swells the immensity of silence to the glorious music, the choir pouring forth notes that range from the adult male's ground-hovering bass to a boy's heaven-piercing soprano. Visual beauty thus reinforced by either deep silence or music makes the cathedral interior a plausible simulacrum of heaven.

The medieval cathedral appealed to me for another reason: there aesthetics merged with ethics, beauty with good. A troubling point with monumental buildings in premodern times was who built them. Answer: the common people, and they did so under more or less severe constraint. One need only think of the deaths and the sufferings of conscripted workers and of draft animals in the construction of Versailles. Cathedrals of the twelfth and thirteenth centuries enjoyed, however, the distinction of being "the first vast monuments in all history to be built by free—nay, unionized!—labor."⁹ As Chartres rose from the ground, Robert of Torigni reported glowingly that 1,145 men and women, both noble and common, had together dedicated all their physical resources and spiritual strength to the task of transporting materials in hand-drawn carts for the construction of the towers.¹⁰

But this is not all. All those who love the cathedral as I do know at the back of their mind that although the cathedral owes its simulation of heavenly splendor far more to the Book of Revelation than to the Gospels, it is nevertheless the simple message of the Gospels—namely, God came down to earth, was humiliated and crucified, to redeem human beings—that, in the ultimate analysis, gives the house of God a transcendent beauty that is inseparable from good.

As a child in China, I read stories that made me long for beauty, truth, and goodness—for a larger world beyond the village that would stimulate my mind and nurture my ideals. Sadly, the older I grew and the deeper I penetrated that world, the more disillusioned I became. Great nature was indeed splendid, but social reality left much to be desired. It was not so much harsh as dull, vain, and false. My parents, I am glad to report, received good grades in my childish, judgmental eyes. They (I could see) did their best to act as they preached, had an admirable sense of social justice, were kind beyond the bounds of family, and demonstrated their contempt for material wealth by having very little of it. But they were nevertheless obliged to compromise with social reality.

In the period of 1942 to 1946, Father was a consular officer in Sydney. His subordinates, I noticed, found all sorts of excuses to offer him gifts. I also noticed that Father himself offered gifts to visiting officials, the quality and expense of which were geared to the visitor's rank. I asked him why all this was necessary. It seemed more than a little undignified. Father patiently explained. Looking back, I can see that he gave me a polished lesson in modern sociology. Society, he said, was structured on relationships of power, which gift exchanges ceremonially affirmed. No doubt other semaphores—such as graded gestures of deference—could be used, but they would be less efficient and even more onerous. One could opt out of society, but one would only end up in another that has its own rungs of power and prestige, its own devices of command and submission.

What a dreary picture of the real world was laid out before me! If I had really believed that there was no more to it than that, I would have lost my motivation for studying and learning. What would be the point of filling my head with glory, when, as an adult, I would be forced to lead a grubby life of calculation, geared to social advancement? But where could I turn for an alternative viewpoint—for rumors of other realities, other modes of being?

The middle school we attended in Sydney—Cranbrook—was affiliated with the Church of England. Headmaster and chaplain conducted religious services that all students were obliged to attend. My brothers and I sat woodenly through them. After a year of exposure to English, we knew the language well enough to understand the sermon as a story, but its point continued to elude us. One day, our form master (a Mr. Roland) called us into his study. We stood before his desk. He wore his academic gown and was seated in a big leather chair. There, he undertook to explain Christianity in half an hour. I, for one, could hardly credit my ears. This symbol of authority was telling us stories about feeding five thousand people with a small basket of food, walking on water, and even of a man who managed to return to life after death. He also told us something that I was looking for. In the Kingdom of God, the first shall be last, the last first, the proud humbled, the humble elevated.

So there was an alternative! Father's secular sociology could be turned on its head. Outwardly unbelieving, inwardly I swallowed the Christian fable whole. Deep down, I wanted a world that did not rest so heavily on power and prestige, and I wanted a physical reality that allowed a tiny hole through which the hint of another reality could enter. I chafed at social convention and was repelled by the exclusivity of kinship favors and preferences. To a rebellious child raised in Chinese familism, Christianity's extraordinary appeal lay in its disrespect for family. Informed that his mother and brothers were asking for him, Jesus said, "Who is my mother? Who are my brothers?" And looking at the people gathered around him, he said, "Here are my mother and my brothers. Whoever does the will of God is my brother, my sister, my mother" (Mark 3:31–35). And who is my neighbor—the next best thing to family? Not necessarily the guy next door, someone I help because he is in a position to help me in return, but rather a total stranger by the roadside whom I may never see again.

Although I didn't know it at the time, my insurrection was not just against the family but against the traditional way of life, rooted in kinship, soil, and earth deities, in favor of the ideals and beliefs of modern life— universal brotherhood, abstract intellection, and a distant sky god, if there is a god. I was growing up, ready to move from hearth to cosmos. Christianity suited my needs, for, though an old religion, its moral doctrines were well ahead of their time. Just think of its abstract universalisms, its insistence that in fundamental dignity there was no difference between Jew and Greek, free and enslaved, men and women; its notion that generosity should be like the sun, which shone impartially on the just and the unjust. Such injunctions were quite impractical (except to a handful of saints) until a time when, as in the Western world, material affluence gave a substantial number of citizens the confidence and the means to practice them, tentatively and sporadically.

Still, I wonder about my vehemence. After all, many young people have made the move from home to world, hearth to cosmos, without disowning the family shrine and its presiding spirits. So why my angry denial of them? I suspect that the answer lies again in my sexual bent, which rules out my having a direct role in maintaining the family line. My fate is to be single. In preliterate or folk communities, such a state is an abomination. An unmarried man or woman is a freak, possibly a witch. Even in the China of my childhood, the imperative to reproduce, to maintain the lineage, makes anyone who fails to contribute beyond the pale. Is it any wonder, then, that I turn to Christianity, or to Buddhism and Stoicism, universalist ideals that define manhood by some other standard? Or, for that matter, to the modern secular world, in which the reproductive function is not viewed idolatrously and in which the single state is acceptable? Indeed, in universal religions and philosophies and in the modern secular world, the single state may be a vocation—a pastoral calling of impartiality toward all God's creatures, or an intellectual calling of total commitment to a field of knowledge—a Paul Erdös (the modern mathematician) who, as Christ of old, had nowhere to lay his head.

As a small child I wanted to be good. By early manhood I pretty much gave up that ambition and wanted, instead, something far more modest, namely, to know what being good meant. I had wisely realized that *being* good could be bad for my health. But as an intellectual question it was safe enough and well worth exploring. Since then I have made my position even safer by subtly shifting the question from "What does it mean to be good?" to "What does a good life mean?" The latter question is not only more impersonal but more geographical. It is also the sort of question that just about everyone asks. In conversation worldwide the three most popular topics are likely to be personal well-being, politics—that is, how society might be improved—and weather, the aspect of nature on which all living things depend and over which even the most advanced technological society has little control.

Now, where does geography enter? Geography enters by way of a new enriched conception of place. The attention that philosophers give to "good life" is given by geographers to "good place."[11] This is possible because places are far more than tangible structures of brick and stone;

they are also synecdoches of human individuals and groups, they constitute human relationships, they embody human strivings and aspirations.

If the basic elements of the good life are widely shared, so are those of the good place. Even the words used to describe them differ little. So, how would one characterize a good place? Inescapably, it seems to me, one would have to include phrases such as fair weather, a lovely natural setting that is also rich in resources, and an architectural world that not only ingratiates the senses but also promotes warm human relationships and individual well-being. These are, however, generalities. What happens if we try to be more specific? Differences of opinion will arise—unless we reach so far back into prehistory that specific ways of life still differed little in essentials. In paleolithic times, for example, because almost everyone was occupied with hunting and/or gathering, the places that supported it—resource-rich areas and campsites—could be measured and ranked against a common standard. By neolithic times, places were already diverse and incompatible—in addition to camps and campsites, farms, nucleated villages, and towns had come into existence. A neolithic philosopher might well wonder whether "good place" could be measured by a single set of characteristics. In the modern period, place diversity increased to encompass wide-ranging types of farms and villages, suburbs, towns, and cities. Incommensurate qualities hit the eye: the "good" in a farm cannot be the "good" in a city.

In our time, *good* is widely considered a relative term. "Good for what? And good in respect to what qualities?" are the proper questions to raise. As the cliché goes, one cannot compare apples and oranges. Yet one can always argue that it is better to have both apples and oranges than to have just apples or just oranges. It is better to live in a time when one can have, if not actually, then imaginatively, the unique taste and texture of both apples and oranges than in a time when only apples existed. This line of reasoning—more is better than less, later is better than earlier—allows good to be compared and ranked. Good, for human beings, is tied to their potential and its degree of realization. The potential in each individual—what he or she can *be, do, experience*—is enormous.

How enormous is suggested by what humans have already accomplished. Take movement through space again. There was a time when a steppe nomad could only walk or run. After the domestication of the horse, another dimension of speed—another way to experience space, more liberating and exhilarating than pumping one's own legs—was his. Today the nomad can ride a horse or a Harley-Davidson motorcycle or get into an airplane and soar into three-dimensional space. I have already rhapsodized over interior space and so will not repeat myself here. But I cannot help adding this: I feel a little sorry for the people who lived before me—for the ancient Egyptian who couldn't have imagined what it would be like to stand in the middle of Hadrian's Pantheon and for the great emperor Hadrian himself, because, all his riches notwithstanding, he couldn't have known in his wildest dreams the beauty (aesthetic and moral) to be found in the interior of Chartres Cathedral.

In moral good too I see progress—not in the sense that human beings have become morally better over time but rather that they *can* become better if they so choose. If even that is too strong, I will take my stand on the modest assertion that they can know more fully what being morally better means as history unfolds. How? Most simply, the answer is the multiplying of sources of inspiration, whether in articulated philosophies or in human lives. It must have been difficult for a person to fulfill his potential for goodness, or even know fully what good could mean, if he lived before, say, 500 B.C.—that is, before Socrates, Buddha, and Confucius had lived and before their systems of moral value were established. And for all the brilliance of these early exemplars, others followed (from Jesus to Gandhi) who continued to add to the repertoire of human goodness.

At its most intimate, moral good is that which transpires between individuals. But first there must be individuals! And, as we have noted, they are largely a creation of the modern era. Of course, there were reflective and self-aware individuals in the past and they could have lived almost anywhere, but they were the rare exceptions. For them to be fairly common, certain conditions must be met. Perhaps the most basic of these is a level of material sufficiency that diminishes the need for bonding and mutual cooperation in the interest of day-to-day survival. Given material sufficiency, people are not only freer to withdraw but will have the space to withdraw into. In rooms designed for privacy, individuals can read a book, pause from time to time to ponder how the world it depicts intersects with the happiness and sorrow, the moral challenges and dilemmas, of their own life. A self thus enriched and self-aware is in the position to offer herself to another in sustained conversation. The result is friendship—true understanding between two individuals and a journey together into life and world, exploring rather than just surviving in it, that distinguishes friendship from the (perhaps) more intense but narrower bonds of kinship, comradeship, and sexual union.[12]

Material sufficiency is not only a condition of intimate morality; it also undergirds impersonal morality, making it possible for even ordinary people to act like the sun that dispenses its genial warmth to all and sundry. Traditional or folk morality is neither intimate (as in friendship of the kind

I have just described) nor impersonal and impartial. It is quintessentially local, for only those who are geographically close can be of assistance in times of need. Need, immediate and dire, dictates the morality of mutual help: I give you a cup of sugar, you give me a cup of vinegar, I help you haul in the harvest, you help me build my barn. Of course, affection—even pure generosity—plays a role, but in communities that have no bins of surplus to fall back on, a truly generous gesture would be heroic and few people are self-sacrificing heroes.

Apart from survival value, tight reciprocity in the local place is immensely attractive, especially to modern men and women, because it is—or can be—warmly human, a consequence of the need to be in constant *direct* touch with kin and neighbor, and because it is modest in its aspiration. Communal morality doesn't make excessive demands on the individual, unlike personal morality in the cultivation of true friendship, or impersonal morality (*caritas*), which requires one to be generous to all—strangers, even enemies.

To the extent that people have become more affluent and secure, communal bonds loosen, narrow reciprocity gives way to or is supplemented by what Lewis Hyde calls "circular" giving. *A* gives to *B* who gives to *C* who gives to *D* who gives to *A*. Generosity is eventually recompensed but only after a long delay, and it will not come from the individual to whom one has given.[13] In an affluent modern society, the circle of giving may be so large that it cannot be encompassed by direct experience. What occurs is linear—a long line that extends into a distant future inhabited by strangers.

No doubt we can all dip into our own life experience and call up instances of the exceptional kindness of strangers. Here is a favorite of mine. I was flying from Denver to Boston. Somewhere over Illinois we were served lunch. I had just finished mine when a voice came over the intercom asking whether a doctor was on the plane. It would appear that a passenger had choked on her food, vomited, and couldn't breathe. A young intern offered help. I leaned over my seat to find an old woman stretched out on the aisle and the young man lying on top of her as though in a lover's embrace. He was trying to suck the vomit out of her mouth and throat. Watching, I became a little nauseous myself. The captain announced that we were making an unscheduled landing in Chicago. An ambulance waited on the landing strip. The woman was taken off the plane, together with the intern, who accompanied her to the hospital. We waited more than an hour for him to return. No one complained. Everyone was sympathetic. We welcomed the young man back as a hero. Before the incident we were all strangers to one another. During it a vague sense of communality emerged.

But in the end we remained strangers. It is most unlikely that the woman would ever have a chance to thank the intern—or for that matter, the solicitous attendants, the patient other passengers, the driver of the ambulance—the whole apparatus of contemporary civilization. But it was precisely the impersonality of the actions—done without chest thumping, almost as a matter of course—that I found inspiring.

With that incident over Chicago in mind, I began to wonder about all the day-to-day acts of selflessness in modern life. These are far more common than fashionable cynicism permits us to acknowledge. In their own quiet way, they are as impressive as the airplane drama. What sorts of acts do I have in mind? Well, an example would be a social worker whose help to her client reaches well beyond her job description. That client, out of gratitude, helps someone else. The favor the social worker does is thus not returned. True, for all kinds of services, money is paid. But the relation between the amount paid and the service rendered is seldom clear. What is the appropriate recompense for an inspiring teacher, or a firefighter who constantly risks her life? Moreover, the amount we pay (a measure of the time and energy taken out of a life) is necessarily very little compared with the goods and services received. What we receive at a department store, an art museum, or a hospital is the accumulated labor, skill, and knowledge of a host of total strangers, most of whom are dead.

May this be a reason that we moderns seldom offer respect to our ancestors or even acknowledge their existence? The usual reason given is that we lack piety, that we are too selfishly absorbed in present and future projects to bother with the past. This may be so, but I believe that another reason may also be at work, and it is one that puts us in a better light. I am saying that we do not acknowledge our ancestors because to do so will take too long. We have too many ancestors, and they have given us far too many good things (from flush toilets to bypass surgery, from sonnets to human rights) for us to be able to even hint at the degree of our indebtedness. By comparison, members of preliterate or folk communities are less burdened. They can show gratitude to their ancestors for passing on to them certain key agricultural skills, social customs, religious rites, and still have time left over for the practical chores of living.

"Salvation by Geography" is not just a catchy chapter title. Geography has directed my attention to the world, and I have found there, for all the inanities and horrors, much that is good and beautiful. The near total neglect of the good is an egregious fault of critical social science, making even its darkest findings, paradoxically, less dark, if only because they are not contrasted with the bright lights that also make up the human picture. In my classes even more than in my books, I have shown, without quite intending to, a pride in human accomplishments and an optimism for the future that surprise many students, for they are at odds with the stories of imperialism, racism, sexism, economic exploitation, hegemony, injustice, and nature degradation that are the standard fare of many courses in cultural studies and human geography. But because this is an autobiography, I am obliged to ask whether a generally upbeat mood concerning the world carries over to my own life. Has my own life been, on the whole, a happy one? Is it, in any sense, a good life?

6

A Good Life?

O N DECEMBER 5, 1998, I turned sixty-eight. I can hardly believe
that my life, up to that point, was such smooth sailing. Naturally,
I have known bad days, months, and even one whole year. But
where are the serious sicknesses and catastrophes—heart attack, hospital-
ization, alcoholism, divorce, death of a child—that bring shadows, touches of cold realism, into even successful and sunny lives? And even if I
have somehow managed to escape bad accidents and nature's disorders, I
surely couldn't have escaped the harshness of society, for society rests on
power, subtly or brutally exercised, a viewpoint that my father imparted to
me long ago and that was confirmed much later in social-science texts.

Might the explanation be that I spent my entire adult life in a university? My two brothers, both academics, have assured me that life there
is no soft perch. A skeptical and even conspiratorial view of university
life can find support among student politicians who claim to be exploited workers, junior faculty who feel oppressed by senior faculty,
senior faculty who feel harassed by administrators, and so on. Much of
this, which I pick up from the campus culture around me, I am prepared
to believe. But my own experience is otherwise. I have not personally
felt the heavy hand of the academic hierarchy. Quite the contrary. At
Berkeley the other grad students and I were confronted by what we
jovially called the sacred triad—Sauer, Leighly, and Kesseli. They were
formidable figures—Olympians, in our eyes—but I never thought of
them as anything other than kindly backers of my aspirations and career. As junior faculty at Indiana University and then at the University of
New Mexico, I was either obtuse or just too full of my own worth to
consider the possibility that I might be exploited. True, my year at the
University of Toronto (1966–1967) was unhappy. It still leaves a sour
taste, but the cause was not bad treatment but intellectual incompatibil-

ity. The fourteen years at the University of Minnesota were wonderful, warm as the summers and stimulating as the winters of the upper Midwest. My colleagues both within the department and beyond seemed to go out of their way to accommodate me. I was never asked to serve on onerous time-consuming committees. In the department I escaped the chores of chairmanship. In the university I was put on the University Press Committee and the Ford Lectureship Committee—two of the most coveted on campus, for the one offered free books, the other free dinner with the visiting lecturer.

And at U.W.–Madison, where I spent the next fourteen years? Let me put it this way. Right from the start, it provided me with an excuse to tell the following story concerning the wit of the archbishop of Canterbury, William Temple (1881–1944), one of my heroes. A wealthy supporter of the church—let's call her Mrs. Murray Montague-Smith—visited the archbishop in his office. The archbishop rose in greeting, "Ah, Mrs. Smith, I am glad to see you. Please take a chair." Whereby, the lady drew up to her full height and said indignantly, "Mrs. *Montague*-Smith, if you please." "Oh," the archbishop replied, "In that case, take two chairs."[1]

In my second year at U.W., I somehow found myself occupying two professorial chairs, one supported by the graduate school, the other by the Vilas Trust. I saw myself a male Mrs. Murray Montague-Smith, though I hope I was not quite so fatuous. As the end of my teaching career approached, I dreamed of slipping quietly into retirement, with no fuss of any kind, except perhaps a small dinner that I would host. Instead, former students Paul Adams, Steven Hoelscher, and Karen Till organized four special sessions in my honor at the Boston meeting of the Association of American Geographers. This was followed by another set of special events at the university, organized by faculty colleagues, staff, and students, that included a reception at the chancellor's residence, a symposium, and a banquet.

A scholar wishes, above all, for intellectual fulfillment. Minnesota and Wisconsin have provided me with a superb environment to do what is in me to do. Over a period of twenty-eight years, I have managed to complete my lifework on systematic humanistic geography: it is made up of ten books, the first of which is *Topophilia* (1974) and the last *Escapism* (1998). As I contemplated retirement in the mid-1990s, friends said encouragingly that I would enjoy another burst of creativity. But this cannot be, for my talent—such as it is—has been used up, thanks to society's unstinting support. I still can't quite believe my good fortune. If, in 1956, when I assumed my first job at Indiana, someone had painted this happy outcome, I would have dismissed it as fantasy or mockery. Yet here they are—the books. No matter how far they fall short of my original intention or some abstract ideal, they undeniably exist—a part of the world—for students to ignore or creatively misread. I feel content, fulfilled. So why the question mark after "the good life"?

The last time I had coffee with Tom Boogaart, a graduate student on his way to Belgium to do research, he said almost casually, "Now that you have retired, I can see that you are eager to end your life." I was shaken. I didn't know I was such an open book. Or it might just be that Tom is an exceptionally penetrating reader, for no one else has suspected this morbid streak. Several years ago, I bought *Final Exit* (1991), which is a sort of handbook for "self-deliverance and assisted suicide."[2] Reading it put me in the dumps, for the book made it obvious that suicide is not an option for me. As a child, I thought nothing of sticking a wriggly earthworm with the sharp point of a fish hook. I can't do that now. I find it hard now to swat a fly. If such tiny bundles of life are too alive for me to kill, what about a large warm body, a human being—me? The idea is preposterous. I don't have the guts to jump out of the window or shoot myself with a gun, and, as *Final Exit* makes clear, I don't have the technical competence for the gentler forms of self-destruction.

Who am I? As a book title, it may sound a little too dramatic—rhetorical—for surely I already know the answer. How can I even think of an autobiography, much less begin to write one, unless I already know my story in outline and, here and there, even in detail? Right—yet not quite to the point. For writing itself—above all, autobiographical writing—is or can be cruelly self-revelatory. The title, rhetorical or not, has forced me to attend to the central question. I now know what I previously at best only suspected. Among the things that I now know, the most desolating is this: except for a brief period in childhood, I have been afraid of life.

My timidity in regard to life is most conspicuous in the area of personal relationships. I seldom initiate one because I dread rebuff or, worse, acceptance followed by betrayal. Even in the relative vigor of early adulthood, I was content to be passive—to just bathe in my companions' good nature and their readiness to accommodate me in their midst. But I was aware that I never could be one of them. My associate status, I thought, had to do with my being younger than they. I was only seventeen when I entered Oxford, whereas the others were in their twenties and many were war veterans of considerable worldly sophistication. I was twenty when I entered Berkeley, the youngest among geography grad students, several of whom were married and had children. It seemed natural that I couldn't fully belong.

A Good Life?

What exactly was my relationship with the other students in California? Consider the monthlong soil-science field course that I took in 1952. The course was a sort of initiation rite—physically, though not mentally, tough. The students in the course—and the instructors too—tended to unbutton, use uncouth language, and horse around, as we worked and camped in proximity to one another week after week. Besides the rough-housing, the physicality of the course was manifested in such necessary activities as putting up and taking down tents, cooking, driving over rugged mountain roads, digging hundreds of holes with the soil auger, and opening and closing numerous gates that led into farms and ranches. All the chores were new to me. Some I couldn't do for lack of skill, others for lack of physical strength: among the latter were digging into hardpan soils and handling the gates efficiently. I was humbled but also touched by the way the other students quietly took the auger out of my hand and finished the work I couldn't manage or when one of them would somehow ease me out of the seat next to the station wagon's front door so that he, not I, would have to jump out to open and close the heavy gates.

I was treated like a younger brother who tagged along—or, a more disturbing thought, like a sister—for I noticed that my coworkers tended to tone down their language (occasionally foul) in my presence. Although I was still new to the country in 1952, I learned in the course of that summer field trip that I could never be at ease when surrounded day and night by young American males. I felt intensely an outsider. What excluded me was not their race or culture but their gender—their self-assured maleness.

Most people have to hide their dislike in the interest of social harmony. I am among those who have to hide their affection for the same end. Not feeling free to show what is, after all, a positive emotion can be hugely oppressive. I became shy and withdrawn. But let me not exaggerate. In youth and early middle age, I was too consumed by the prose and poetry of the world to mope. I was alone and unattached. All right, so be it. I would have more time and energy to read, think, and, above all, daydream and reflect.

Only much later, as the whispers of mortality grew louder with each decade added to my age, did I begin to question seriously a life so devoid of anything like mutual and exclusive attachment. When I look around, I discover the commonplace but to me amazing fact that almost all human beings have at least one individual to whom they owe their primary loyalty and love and from whom they can expect loyalty and love in return. It could be a spouse, a child, a lover, an intimate friend, or a group such as the family. I cannot remember ever having had such a person or group. When,

Fig. 15. With Steven Hoelscher at Disneyland, California, June 1995.

late in life, I do have someone to myself for a brief period, socially or even professionally, I tend to romanticize the occasion, giving it greater import than it perhaps merits. Love, when frustrated, degenerates into sentimentality, a weakness that I fight against but with little success.

Here is a case in point. In June 1995 I went with Steven Hoelscher, then a U.W. graduate student, to Disneyland to do (believe it or not) fieldwork for the Canadian Centre for Architecture.[3] We were there for three days. Dawn broke one morning with hard and persistent rain, forcing us to stay in the motel and wait for it to stop. When the rain continued into the afternoon, we decided to take a bus to Disneyland and explore its indoor shows. We had to endure more waiting, this time for the bus. Now, if I had been alone, my stomach would have churned in frustration and my mind would have drifted into unhealthy directions such as why I was at Disneyland and, for that matter, what I was doing in Wisconsin, in the United States, on earth. But with Steve beside me, I felt at peace (see fig. 15). Being with him was in itself sufficient purpose, sufficient goal. I marveled at the thought that out of six million people in the greater Los Angeles area, the one individual I preferred to be with was right beside me. I also indulged in the thought that the same might be true for Steve, because he had told me that he didn't know anyone in this part of California. And so, within a narrow time period and a strictly defined geographical area, I could be number one to another human being.

When did I first become conscious of my second-class status? As a child, you remember, I was sensitive to not being first in my parents' eyes. But many children probably want to be extraspecial to at least one parent or grown-up. They outgrow this need—this dependency—as I did. However, I went too far. I gave up intimate human relationships altogether in favor of the beauty of the world, that is, geography. As gray exceeded black in the coloring of my hair, I was haunted by an immense void. If filling it with a permanent partner was out of the question, as it seemed to be, I yearned for friendship—for individuals who, at least in the moments we were together, could give me the illusion of having their undivided attention, of being (in that sense) their "number one." Happily, in Minneapolis, such individuals—my departmental colleagues—were there for me next door. Several were older than I, which meant that their children, already teenagers, no longer needed their vigilant care. My older colleagues were thus free to be themselves: they were their proper names, not just generic fathers and husbands. I felt this most strongly in the presence of Phil Porter. When I talked with Phil over the tea that I brewed in my office, I saw him as a contained individual who was wholly there for me as I was for him.

Besides colleagues, I also enjoyed the friendship of a few graduate students, especially that of John Hickey. I took his friendship so much for granted that in 1974 I casually asked, "Hey, John, what about helping me drive to Davis, California, in my VW Beetle?" Without batting an eyelid, John said, "Sure." This meant three days on the road, and John would have to fly back to Minneapolis on his own. A year later, he flew out to Davis and drove my Beetle back alone across two thirds of the continent, so that I could return the easy and quick way by plane. I remember feeling grateful to John at the time. In retrospect, how insufficient that gratitude was, for I now see his willingness to help over a span of days as a miracle of generosity.[4]

When I came to Madison in 1983, I found myself in a much younger department. My colleagues were in their early forties and had young families that consumed their time and energy outside of teaching and research. In their company, I often noticed a certain wariness, a need to keep an eye on the clock. The time they had for me was contingent on the odd opening in a heavily booked family schedule. I learned to seek their company as part of a family outing rather than as individuals. On the rare occasions that I made a personal request—would you come to my public lecture or book reading at Borders?—their answer tended to be equivocal. The pause in the response, the attempt to find some excuse, did not arise from any lack of goodwill. It was rather a question of priorities. Even if the nonworking hours were not already committed to specific domestic chores, they were still best left open for recuperation.

In Madison I soon developed a fondness for my colleagues and their young families. Being Chinese, I took pleasure in my chronological seniority and in the role of elder brother. But friendship—true friendship—was another matter, for in that relationship one must be willing not only to give but to make demands. I was extremely reluctant to make demands. Once in a blue moon, however, desperate need left me little choice. An incident that was traumatic for me occurred a dozen or so years ago. One Saturday afternoon, I was working in my office in Science Hall, as was my habit, but after a while I felt unwell and so returned home. The pinched sensation over my chest and a feeling of nausea persisted. I called my physician but, this being Saturday, he could not be reached. A standby physician answered and, unaware of my medical history, advised me to go to the emergency room right away, for it might be a heart attack. He also said that I must not attempt to drive. I called the various people I knew in Madison, but no one was at home except one, who, however, could not come to my rescue. Over the phone, he said, "I know what you have in mind. You would like me to drive you to the hospital, but I can't because I have a prior engagement."

I can no longer remember what the prior engagement was, and I couldn't at the time show proper appreciation for the help he did give me, which was to make phone calls on my behalf. With the first sign of refusal, I entered into a state of shock, for I had taken for granted that in a life-threatening situation I could certainly count on the help of someone I had gone to lunches and dinners with. Why, even total strangers would respond. Suppose I had called 911—wouldn't I have heard the siren screaming in less than ten minutes and the sound of the feet of young ambulance personnel pounding up the staircase as though their grandfather was dying? I mentioned the incident afterward to Bob Sack, a close friend and colleague. He attempted to show me that our mutual friend's response was entirely reasonable and that generous help was, after all, given me, just not in the form that I had expected. In short, I was being neurotic. I nodded in quasi-agreement. But what I felt was a chill down my spine and a deadening of the atmosphere around me. For the subtextual message I heard was that if Bob had been at home and answered the phone, he too might have found a good reason to say no.

Jim Knox was at home that Saturday afternoon and came to my rescue. He drove me to the emergency room and sat with me for three hours while I underwent various tests. It turned out that my symptoms had nothing to do with a heart attack, although, of course, no one could have known it at the time. Later I thought gratefully that Jim had used up three hours of his life on me—hours that he could have put to better use reading with his daughter, Sarah, or shopping with his wife, Kathy.

I also thought, Suppose I had called Jim first? My expectation would have been met. Would I, as a consequence, have a little more confidence in my worth now—in my worth not as a colleague clothed in health and respectability but as a naked biped, a needy individual? How can a single chance event—calling one friend rather than another—make such a difference? A mature person's sense of his own worth should be more firmly grounded, as mine obviously wasn't. Finally, I wondered about the nature of my fear when the doctor told me to go to the emergency room. Was it really death or something else? I believe that it was something else—the fear of being totally alone, the anxiety about my utter incompetence in the world of the hospital, the sudden plunge into meaninglessness. The questions that flooded into my mind as I waited for help were curiously trivial. Where have I put my insurance policy? Do I need to bring a toothbrush? Do I have a clean pair of pajamas? And more seriously, can I bear pain with decent stoicism?

The day after the false alarm was Sunday. I rested and recovered. On Monday, as the lunch hour approached, I went upstairs as usual to join my colleagues in the common room. At the last minute, I found that I couldn't do it. So I ate elsewhere. And I have not been able to eat communally (except in staff meetings and other formal occasions) since. Absenting myself was not a conscious decision. I just lacked the fortitude to encounter friendly faces in the common room, for they could again lead me into expectations that would not—could not—be met.

A recurrent theme in this autobiography is my lack of vitality. Vitality is expressed in the taking of physical and emotional risks—in skydiving, in demands for love that risk rejection that too is a sort of death. But, as the cliché goes, nothing ventured, nothing gained. What is gained is, of course, the warm glow of life. Perhaps I have a bit more vitality than some people—Alfred Russel Wallace's younger brother, for instance. Nevertheless, I feel keenly my inferiority. How inferior, how timid, I know in sorrow and regret—infinite regret because it is far too late to do anything about it—when I compare myself with someone brave and vigorous like John Cheever, the novelist. He loved well, at times heedlessly, and demanded that others love him in return. He did and had everything that I could do and have only in puerile fantasy.

"When I was a young man," Cheever wrote, "I woke one morning in the unclean bedsheets of a squalid furnished room, poor and hungry and lonely, and thought that some morning I would wake in my own house, holding in my arms a fragrant bride and hearing from the broad lawn beyond my window the voices of my beloved children. *And so I did*" (emphasis added). He wrote of connubial bliss. He waited with his children in the woodland for his wife to come into view. "Her shoulders are bare; her dress is cut low. She carries an armful of lilies, trailing this way and that their mournful perfume. She seems content and so am I and when she takes my arm and we continue to walk under the trees in the last light, under the beeches that spray like shrapnel, arm in arm, after so many years and with so much sexual ardor I think we are like two sheltered by the atmosphere of some campus; that we are like a couple engraved on a playing card."

His tenderest entries in a journal published posthumously in 1991 are of his children. Here is one among many about Frederico, when he was three years old. "Walk with my youngest son in the sun. How my whole love of life seems to gather around his form; how he fills me with the finest ambitions." Here is a rather long and rhapsodic entry about his older son, Ben:

> It is after dark—just. A summer night, stars and fireflies. . . . My older son stands on the bridge over the brook with a Roman candle. He is a man now. His voice is deep. He is barefoot and wears chinos. It takes two or three matches to light the fuse. There is a splutter of pink fire, a loud hissing. . . . The light changes from pink to green, from green to red. It makes on the trees and in the heavy air an amphitheatre or sphere of unearthly light. In this I see his beloved face, his figure. I cannot say truthfully that I have never felt anything but love for him. We have quarreled, he has wet his bed. . . . But all of this is gone. Now there is nothing between us but love and good-natured admiration.

Cheever was bisexual. He desired women, but he also desired men, even though he knew that every handsome delivery boy or waiter was like a gun held to his head. One of his deep homosexual longings was to be taken care of. He dreamed of lying in the arms of a man who "will pay the bills, the taxes, balance the checking account and drive the car through the storm." But it wasn't just a dream. Cheever had the courage to make it come true. He had a lover who offered to help him check out of the hospital. "He is twenty minutes late," Cheever wrote, "but when he arrives he packs my things, oversees my departure from the hospital with tenderness and dispatch, points out interesting changes on the drive home while gently caressing my leg, and upon our return removes my clothes, washes and changes my bloody dressing, and delights and engorges my sexuality."

Cheever had more than his share of love, lust, and tenderness. Yet he never felt he had enough. On numerous occasions, he found tenderness with his children. Yet he spoke as though that emotion rarely came his way and that the least sign of it was a miracle. "What is this mysterious need? In a crowded Roman trolley car at closing time on a winter night, someone touches me by chance on the shoulder. I do not turn to see who it is and I will never know if it was a man or a woman, a tart or a priest, but the gentle touch excites in me such longing for a sort of helpful tenderness that I sigh; my knees are weak."[5]

As I read his complaint, repeated over and over again in the journal, I feel the anger that a half-starved peasant might feel toward his lord who complains of an insufficiency of pigeon meat on a table groaning with food.

Half-starved peasant I might be in matters of love and attachment, but I do have my crumbs, which are delicious—deficient only in size, not in quality. Here are two that I have saved for the long wintry days ahead.

I had planned to have dinner with Bob and Karen Sack to mark my birthday on December 5, 1988. But they both caught the flu. I spent the day working in the office as usual and was just about to leave when the phone rang. I picked it up to hear the small hesitant voice of a boy asking whether I would go out and have dinner with him. It was Joshua, the Sacks' ten-year-old son. He had assumed the responsibility of giving me my birthday treat. And so I went to his home and we two then trudged through the snow to a neighborhood restaurant on Monroe Street. Joshua was an exceptionally handsome boy, and I noticed that he had brushed and slicked back his great mop of hair in honor of the occasion (see fig. 16). We sat down to eat at our little table in the crowded restaurant. Heads turned furtively in our direction, sometimes with a quizzical smile. Our neighbors must have wondered: "What is going on here? The man obviously is not the child's grandfather. And he doesn't look like a babysitter. What is their relationship? What can they talk about?" Well, Joshua politely inquired how I was and then proceeded to tell me about mountain glaciation in Vermont, where he had spent the summer in his grandmother's cabin.

Over the years, I have told this story a number of times and I have even managed to write it up for an article that was published in 1989.[6] Far from fading as the years go by, it gains significance. For example, only now, as I write this section, the thought occurs to me that I was very probably Joshua's first candlelight dinner date. What a privilege! Still, it may seem strange—even a little sad—that a man of my age and experience, looking back on a long past, should remember, so vividly, this dinner with a kid. The event has charm, certainly, but people may reasonably ask, "Haven't

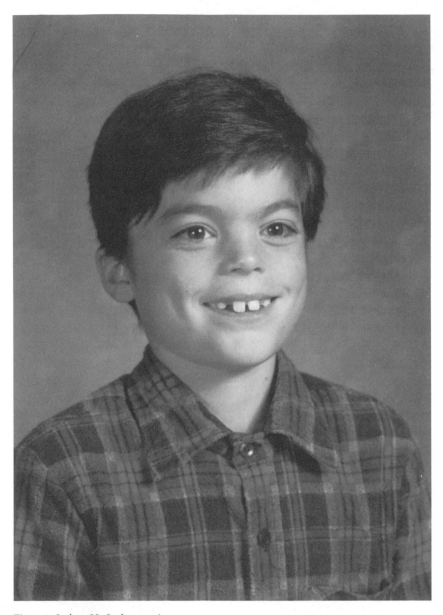

Fig. 16. Joshua H. Sack, age nine.

Fig. 17. Convocation at the University of Waterloo, Canada, when I was awarded an honorary doctoral degree in environmental science, May 21, 1985.

there been more momentous occasions for you? What about the applause after one of your more successful speeches? What about the flattering notice in the *Chronicle of Higher Education*? What about the moment when the president of the University of Waterloo bestowed on you an honorary degree?" (see fig. 17).

Well, yes, I am glad to have had these successes, and they were certainly important to me at the time. But they have no power to stir me now: they are quite useless when I need something to console me in a dark mood. And if they nevertheless linger in the shadows of my memory cave, it is because my employer requires that I keep track of them as part of my official record. From this, I gain the following happy, but totally unoriginal, thought—unoriginal because it merely confirms folk wisdom. What gives deep satisfaction in life is made up of quite ordinary experiences— "ordinary," however, only through a failure of the imagination—that we "plain folk" are as likely to have as the wealthy, the famous, and the talented. There may be more justice in the world, a fairer distribution of the goods that matter, than I thought.

My second precious crumb came almost a decade later. After more than forty years of teaching, I gave my last class on December 12, 1997. I collected student journals for the course "Space and Place." Several included a personal comment. One student, Peter Prohaska, wrote:

I hope it will not seem intrusive to your sense of place and home that my roommate, who is also taking this course, and I noticed one warm fall evening that you lived right across the street from us. It seemed a particularly fortuitous twist of fate that our chance to take a course on "Space and Place" from such an eminent figure should coincide with our finding a house in such a proximate place. It served us well within the context of the class because our other friends were interested to know that our professor lived across the way, and we had to explain and discuss the course content, especially the issues that arose from this serendipity. Even as I write this, I know that familiar ringed lamp is lit, perhaps shedding light on some erudite work of anthropologic literature. It was a rare bit of luck that even as I consider the sense of shelter in a storm, the makings of a place, what a home may be . . . and even as I read C. S. Lewis or [your book] *Morality and Imagination,* I was privileged to think that perhaps across the way some affirming nod might accompany my cogitations, that some affinity between teacher and pupil beyond that of the classroom may be formed, whether acknowledged or not. I hope that you will read these lines as they are meant . . . sincere thanks for projecting such an authentic feeling of desire that we as students might come to understand better the aspects of the world which are in need of the thought and concern with which you have nurtured them.

I invited Peter Prohaska and his roommate, Lindy Nelson, for dinner at our neighborhood restaurant, Wilson Street Grill. Strange isn't it—or natural because of my rootlessness—that the most precious and dearest moments in my life are more likely to occur in a coffee shop or restaurant than in the bedroom or the kitchen alcove? My dependence on public places and on chance or transitory encounters for emotional fulfillment forces me to conclude that I am immature. I have skipped two critical stages of life—marriage and parenthood. I have grown old without having grown up. I have missed both the crushing weight and the uplifting joy of biological propagation and family responsibility. The one consolation I have is that immaturity is a signal trait of our species.

Immaturity is the feeling of never being quite in place, truly at home. We envy animals in part because they, unlike us, all look so much at home in their natural habitat. Our tendency is to outgrow whatever we have, not only our natural habitat but also protective shells of our own making, from shoes and houses to ideas. Human stages of maturation take so long that we are used to being young, used to the idea that we will change. Animals, by contrast, pass through youth so quickly that it is as though their destiny is to be mature—adult, well adjusted, and stable. Human stories can be bewildering because their characters seem fluid. By contrast, animal stories are comforting because their characters—Badger, Mole, Rat, Toad—seem fixed, true to type.

By nature never quite at home, humans continually strive for stability by building homes. Social convention is such a home. Children are taught how to live in it. Yet one of their charms is their obliviousness to convention, occasionally saying and doing things that are touched with originality. Older children sometimes deliberately defy adult convention with conventions of their own—dying their hair green or pink, for instance. At another scale and level, sociopolitical revolutions are defiances of convention by conventional means, that is, by the set practices (marches, slogans, and so on) of revolutionary movements.

The acts of the greatest appeal to me are not, however, these group acts of defiance—these collective manifestations of "immaturity," important as they surely are—but rather individual, playful, often non-self-conscious acts of deviance, the type of deviance that is another name for originality. A major reason that my dinner with young Joshua so enchanted me was its departure from norm. If I had been his grandfather and the birthday was Joshua's, the dinner would still have been enjoyable—even memorable— but it would also have been conventional, prescribed and described in some complete book of etiquette. Again, a teacher praising his student is normal; a student praising his teacher with that degree of warmth and eloquence is not. If these examples of deviance seem too personal, perhaps even trivial, let me give a couple that sharply underline the importance of such jeux d'esprit to humanity at its most endearing and best. On a moral plane, consider acts of spontaneous and extraordinary kindness. Isn't there something open, youthful, and heedless about them? In any case, about such acts, neither etiquette books nor moral codes—both works of stabilizing convention—have much to say. On an intellectual plane, think of the deviance of a new insight, the twist on an old one—naughtinesses of a probing (and, in that sense, immature) mind—that can lead to nonparadigmatic achievement.

There is a touch of pride in these claims of immaturity. But also of regret. I yearn at times for a real home, permanence, continuing and dependable (that is, "mature") relationships, and even, in a weak moment, a firm reputation in an established discipline that can boast a long roster of scholars, a building of its own with paneled rooms, time-honored procedures for the granting of awards. But fate has decreed otherwise.

Let me end with an encapsulating anecdote. My memory for facts is not very good, as I have said, so I cannot remember the year or, precisely, the location of this event. It happened, in any case, well before I came to Wisconsin. I was alone, driving west late—well past midnight—across the sparsely settled landscapes of Nebraska. My car and another one ahead were the only two on the narrow highway. We kept each other company. I was never a confident driver, least of all in the dark, so I appreciated the front car's taillights, which guided me and made me feel safe. Just when I was beginning to take my companion for granted, his right-turn signal started to flicker. A friendly gesture, I thought, but also regrettable, because I was going to be left to myself. The car turned into a country lane. Henceforth, I had only my own headlights to show me the way. They illuminated a short stretch of the road and were then absorbed by a wall of darkness.

Notes
Ackowledgments

Notes

CHAPTER 1. AUTOBIOGRAPHY: MY ANGLE

1. Dorothy Lee, "Linguistic Reflection of Wintu Thought," and "The Conception of the Self Among the Wintu Indians," in *Freedom and Culture* (Englewood Cliffs, N.J.: Prentice-Hall, 1959), pp. 121–130, 131–140.

2. Hoyt Alverson, *Mind in the Heart of Darkness: Value and Self-Identity Among the Tswana of Southern Africa* (New Haven, Conn.: Yale University Press, 1978), pp. 68–69.

3. Georges Gusdorf, "Conditions et limites de l'autobiographie," in G. Reichenkron and E. Haase, eds., *Formen der Selbstdarstellung: Analekten zu einer Geschichte des literarischen Selbstportraits* (Berlin: Duncker & Humblot, 1956); Paul Delaney, *British Autobiography in the Seventeenth Century* (London: Routledge & Kegan Paul, 1969), p. 13.

4. Jacquetta Hawkes, *A Land* (London: Cresset, 1951), p. 143.

5. John Wain, *Samuel Johnson: A Biography* (New York: Viking, 1975), p. 43.

6. Leon Radzinowicz, *A History of English Criminal Law and Its Administration from 1750*, vol. 1 (London: Stevens, 1948), p. 216.

CHAPTER 2. WORLD STAGE AND PUBLIC EVENTS

1. This is the topic of my book *Cosmos and Hearth: A Cosmopolite's Viewpoint* (Minneapolis: University of Minnesota Press, 1996).

2. Jonathan D. Spence and Annping Chin, *The Chinese Century: A Photographic History of the Last Hundred Years* (New York: Random House, 1996).

3. My own memory yields little. I draw on the far better memory of my younger brother, San-Fu, for the family facts.

4. My friend and colleague at the University of Wisconsin–Madison, E. David Cronon, was an American officer stationed in Manila in 1946. He too attended the independence ceremony. We may have walked past each other then, but we didn't actually meet until November 1983, when he, as dean of the College of Letters and Science, interviewed me for a position at the university.

5. I acknowledged my father's help in the paper, "A Coastal Reconnaissance of Central Panama," *California Geographer* 3 (1962): 77.

6. Margaret Mead, "Children, Culture, and Edith Cobb," in *Children, Nature, and the Urban Environment: Proceedings of a Symposium Fair,* USDA Forest Service General Technical Report NE-30, 1977, p. 22. Geographer Ward Barrett of the University of Minnesota captured what Margaret Mead meant to people by calling her the "grandmother of the Western world."

CHAPTER 3. PERSONAL: FROM PARENTS TO STONE

1. T. S. Eliot, *The Use of Poetry and the Use of Criticism* (London: Faber and Faber, 1948), p. 148.

2. Gregory Wolfe, *Malcolm Muggeridge: A Biography* (Grand Rapids, Mich.: Eerdmans, 1997), p. 24.

3. I was glad to have the opportunity to pay homage to desert and ice in an article called "Desert and Ice: Ambivalent Aesthetics," in Salim Kemal and Ivan Gaskell, eds., *Landscape, Natural Beauty, and the Arts* (Cambridge: Cambridge University Press, 1993), pp. 139–157.

4. Yi-Fu Tuan, "A Coastal Reconnaissance of Central Panama," *California Geogapher* 3 (1962): 77–96.

5. William Wordsworth, "Composed upon Westminster Bridge, September 3, 1802," *Selected Poems* (London: Penguin, 1994), p. 170.

6. John Updike, "The Egg Race," *New Yorker,* June 13, 1977, pp. 36–40.

7. S. L. Washburn and Irven DeVore, "Social Behavior of Baboons and Early Man," in S. L. Washburn, ed., *Social Life of Early Man* (Chicago: Aldine, 1961), p. 101.

CHAPTER 4. INTIMATE: FROM JUSTICE TO LOVE

1. Painful as it was, I did complete my postdoc in statistics.

2. Alfred Russel Wallace, *My Life: A Record of Events and Opinions*, vol. 1 (London: Chapman & Hall, 1905), pp. 281–283.

3. Gerald Brenan, *Thoughts in a Dry Season: A Miscellany* (Cambridge: Cambridge University Press, 1978), p. 84.

4. Skutnick is quoted in the *New Republic*, February 3, 1982. For other examples of this type of heroism, the winners of the Carnegie Medal, see Robert H. Frank, *Passions Within Reason* (New York: Norton, 1988), pp. 212–213.

5. Gregory Wolfe, *Malcolm Muggeridge: A Biography* (Grand Rapids, Mich.: Eerdmans, 1997), p. 353.

6. Michael Ignatieff, review of Isaiah Berlin's "The Crooked Timber of Humanity," *New Republic,* April 29, 1991, p. 33.

7. Michel de Montaigne, *Essays* (Harmondsworth, Middlesex, U.K.: Penguin, 1958), p. 199.

8. Milan Kundera, *Immortality* (New York: Grove Weidenfeld, 1991), p. 21.

9. Tepilit Ole Saitoti, *The Worlds of a Maasai Warrior* (Berkeley: University of California Press, 1988), p. 114.

10. Ashley Montagu, *The Elephant Man: A Study in Human Dignity* (New York: Dutton, 1979), p. 14.

11. John Updike, *Self-consciousness* (New York: Knopf, 1989), p. 251.

12. Alice Adams, "Greyhound People," *New Yorker,* January 19, 1981, p. 40.

13. Ellis Peters, *The Pilgrim of Hate* (New York: Mystery Press Book, 1997), p. 120.

14. Ellis Peters, *The Confessions of Brother Haluin* (New York: Mystery Press Book, 1989), p. 191.

15. Helen Keller, *The World I Live In* (New York: Century, 1908), p. 75.

16. Dorothy Day, *Long Loneliness* (New York: Harper, 1962), p. 148.

17. Helmut de Terra, *Humboldt: The Life and Times of Alexander von Humboldt, 1769–1859* (New York: Knopf, 1955), p. 27.

18. Ibid., 66–67.

19. Douglas Botting, *Humboldt and the Cosmos* (New York: Harper & Row, 1973), pp. 195–197.

20. Yi-Fu Tuan, *Alexander von Humboldt and His Brother: Portrait of An Ideal Geographer in Our Time* (Los Angeles: Department of Geography, University of California, 1997), p. 11.

CHAPTER 5. SALVATION BY GEOGRAPHY

1. This chapter is a greatly expanded version of my Charles Homer Haskins Lecture, "A Life of Learning," American Council of Learned Societies Occasional Paper no. 42, 1998.

2. Paul Lewis, "Too Late to Say 'Extinct' in Ubykh, Eyak or Ona," *New York Times,* August 15, 1998, p. 13.

3. Yi-Fu Tuan, "Island Selves: Human Disconnectedness in a World of Interdependence," *Geographical Review* 85, no. 2 (1995): 237–238.

4. William Styron, *The Confessions of Nat Turner: A Novel* (New York: Random House, 1967), pp. 239–240.

5. Antoine de Saint-Exupéry, *Wind, Sand, and Stars* (Harmondsworth, Middlesex, U.K.: Penguin, 1966), p. 24.

6. *Time,* November 4, 1996, p. 80.

7. Sigfried Giedion, *Architecture and the Phenomena of Transition: The Three Space Conceptions in Architecture* (Cambridge, Mass.: Harvard University Press, 1971).

8. Erwin Panofsky, *Abbot Suger on the Abbey Church of St.-Denis and Its Art Treasures* (Princeton, N.J.: Princeton University Press, 1946), p. 19.

9. Lynn White Jr., *Machina ex Deo* (Cambridge, Mass.: MIT Press 1968), p. 63.

10. Pierre du Colombier, *Les chantiers des cathédrales* (Paris: J. Picard, 1953), p. 18, quoted in Adolf Katzenellenbogen, *The Sculptural Programs of Chartres Cathedral* (New York: Norton, 1964), p. vii.

11. Robert David Sack, *Homo Geographicus: A Framework for Action, Awareness, and Moral Concern* (Baltimore, Md.: Johns Hopkins University Press, 1997).

12. Andrew Sullivan, *Love Undetectable: Notes on Friendship, Sex, and Survival* (New York: Knopf, 1998), pp. 175–252. This is a rare and superb modern essay on the challenges and rewards of friendship, as distinct from other intense or intimate human relationships.

13. Lewis Hyde, *The Gift: Imagination and the Erotic Life of Property* (New York: Vintage, 1983), pp. 11–24; Yi-Fu Tuan, *Morality and Imagination: Paradoxes of Progress* (Madison: University of Wisconsin Press, 1989), pp. 112–113.

CHAPTER 6. A GOOD LIFE?

1. The story comes from a biography of William Temple. Unfortunately, I can't locate its source and so have had to make up the double-barreled name of Mrs. Murray Montague-Smith.

2. Derek Humphrey, *Final Exit: The Practicalities of Self-Deliverance and Assisted Suicide for the Dying* (Eugene, Ore.: Hemlock Society, 1991).

3. Yi-Fu Tuan and Steven D. Hoelscher, "Disneyland: Its Place in World Culture," in Karal Ann Marling, ed., *Designing Disney's Theme Parks: The Architecture of Reassurance* (Paris and New York: Flammarion, 1997), pp. 191–198.

4. I should mention that Jemuel Ripley, in the summer of 1997, drove me from Madison to Minneapolis to spend a day with me at the Mall of America. I had to be there for a research project. Jemuel didn't. Moreover, he had been there before. So he came just to help me out.

5. John Cheever, *The Journals of John Cheever* (New York: Knopf, 1991).

6. I published a version of this story in U.W.–Madison's *L&S Magazine*, Fall 1989, in a piece called "Good Life and Old Age," p. 4. I gather that the magazine is distributed to tens of thousands of alumni. So it may be that this story is more widely read than any other paper or book I have written.

Acknowledgments

I WISH TO THANK first the American Council of Learned Societies for inviting me to deliver the lecture "A Life of Learning," for it stimulated in me a desire to go beyond mere intellectual life to something more complete—this autobiography. The invitation would not have come without diligent canvassing on my behalf by Ronald Abler, the executive director of the American Association of Geographers. So, Ron, my heartfelt thanks.

Having written a draft of the autobiography, I wondered who would be interested in publishing it. To my delight, Mary Elizabeth Braun, an editor with the University of Wisconsin Press, showed keen interest from the start and gave me every encouragement to proceed. Other friends who encouraged me as I labored on were Sally and Lee Hanson and David Lowenthal. Sally and Lee are new friends; I got to know them well in our Saturday morning coffee sessions only in the last few months, but how little length of time matters in friendship! As for David, we first met almost thirty-five years ago in Columbus, Ohio. Ever since, he has been not only a friend but a model and an inspiration. Every copy editor has been a teacher to me, telling me how to spell, write grammatically, and avoid verbosity and fuzziness. I am fortunate to have had excellent teachers. Among them is my current copy editor—Polly Kummel.

I wish to thank my brothers, Tai-Fu and San-Fu, and my sister, Sze-Fu, for supplying me with facts from our childhood. I envy them their good memory. I thank them especially because they were willing to help me despite, I suspect, an uneasy awareness that the completed portrait will show them a brother they barely recognize.

So many people—parents, teachers, siblings, colleagues, and students—have played a role in making me into the sort of person I am. Whatever decency there is in me I owe to them. Many moral weaknesses remain, for which I alone am responsible.

Wisconsin Studies in Autobiography

William L. Andrews
General Editor

Robert F. Sayre
The Examined Self: Benjamin Franklin, Henry Adams, Henry James

Daniel B. Shea
Spiritual Autobiography in Early America

Lois Mark Stalvey
The Education of a WASP

Margaret Sams
Forbidden Family: A Wartime Memoir of the Philippines, 1941–1945
Edited, with an introduction, by Lynn Z. Bloom

Journeys in New Worlds: Early American Women's Narratives
Edited by William L. Andrews

Mark Twain
Mark Twain's Own Autobiography: The Chapters from the North American Review
Edited, with an introduction, by Michael J. Kiskis

American Autobiography: Retrospect and Prospect
Edited by Paul John Eakin

Charlotte Perkins Gilman
The Living of Charlotte Perkins Gilman: An Autobiography
Introduction by Ann J. Lane

Caroline Seabury
The Diary of Caroline Seabury: 1854–1863
Edited, with an introduction, by Suzanne L. Bunkers

Cornelia Peake McDonald
A Woman's Civil War: A Diary with Reminiscences of the War, from March 1862
Edited, with an introduction, by Minrose G. Gwin

Marian Anderson
My Lord, What a Morning
Introduction by Nellie Y. McKay

American Women's Autobiography: Fea(s)ts of Memory
Edited, with an introduction, by Margo Culley

Frank Marshall Davis
Livin' the Blues: Memoirs of a Black Journalist and Poet
Edited, with an introduction, by John Edgar Tidwell

Joanne Jacobson
Authority and Alliance in the Letters of Henry Adams

Kamau Brathwaite
The Zea Mexican Diary: 7 Sept 1926–7 Sept 1986
Foreword by Sandra Pouchet Paquet

Genaro M. Padilla
My History, Not Yours: The Formation of Mexican American Autobiography

Frances Smith Foster
Witnessing Slavery: The Development of Ante-bellum Slave Narratives

Native American Autobiography: An Anthology
Edited, with an introduction, by Arnold Krupat

American Lives: An Anthology of Autobiographical Writing
Edited, with an introduction, by Robert F. Sayre

Carol Holly
Intensely Family: The Inheritance of Family Shame and the Autobiographies of Henry James

G. Thomas Couser
Recovering Bodies: Illness, Disability, and Life Writing

People of the Book: Thirty Scholars Reflect on Their Jewish Identity
Edited by Jeffrey Rubin-Dorsky and Shelley Fisher Fishkin

John Downton Hazlett
My Generation: Collective Autobiography and Identity Politics

William Herrick
Jumping the Line: The Adventures and Misadventures of an American Radical

Women, Autobiography, Theory: A Reader
Edited by Sidonie Smith and Julia Watson

José Angel Gutiérrez
The Making of a Chicano Militant: Lessons from Cristal

Yi-Fu Tuan
Who Am I? An Autobiography of Emotion, Mind, and Spirit

Carson McCullers
Illumination and Night Glare: The Unfinished Autobiography of Carson McCullers
Edited, with an introduction, by Carlos Dews

Marie Hall Ets
Rosa: The Life of an Italian Immigrant

B Tuan

Tuan, Yi-fu, 1930-

Who am I? : an
autobiography of
c1999.